Heritage Studies 6

for Christian Schools®
SECOND EDITION

To Know the Past

Ancient Landmarks

D1501083

Coordinating Writer: Eileen M. Berry

Contributing Writers: Sharon Hambrick, Linda K. Hayner, Kimberly H. Pascoe, Stephanie Ralston, Dawn L. Watkins

Bob Jones University Press, Greenville, South Carolina 29614

Note:
The fact that materials produced by other publishers may be referred to in this volume does not constitute an endorsement of the content or theological position of materials produced by such publishers. Any references and ancillary materials are listed as an aid to the student or the teacher and in an attempt to maintain the accepted academic standards of the publishing industry.

**HERITAGE STUDIES 6 for Christian Schools® Second Edition
To Know the Past: Ancient Landmarks**

Coordinating Writer
Eileen M. Berry

Contributing Writers
Sharon Hambrick
Linda K. Hayner
Kimberly H. Pascoe
Stephanie Ralston
Dawn L. Watkins

Produced in cooperation with the Bob Jones University Department of Social Studies Education, the College of Arts and Science, and Bob Jones Elementary School.

© 1998 Bob Jones University Press
Greenville, South Carolina 29614
First Edition © 1986 Bob Jones University Press

ISBN 1-57924-063-1

15 14 13 12 11 10 9 8 7 6 5

Contents

1   Between Great Rivers: Mesopotamia   1

2   The Gift of the Nile: Ancient Egypt   23

3   The People of One God: Ancient Israel   49

4   Mysteries of the Indus: Ancient India   73

5   Dynasties in Seclusion: Ancient China   97

6   A Glory by the Sea: Classical Greece   119

7   Power of the Seven Hills: Roman World   145

8   Of Jade and Stone: Ancient Mayas   169

9   Story Keepers and Kings: Ancient Africa   191

10   Golden Age of the Orient: Japan, China, India   213

11   Mosaics and Minarets: Byzantine Empire   243

12   Shadow of the Castle: Middle Ages   271

Glossary   295

Index   307

1

Between Great Rivers:
Mesopotamia

The Days of Abraham

Perhaps you have read about Abraham many times and know his story well. But some people doubt his existence—and the truth of most of the Bible. They prefer to trust in science and their own understanding. Scientific discoveries, however, support the Bible accounts.

In the 1850s English explorers proved that an ancient ruin in the Middle East was the biblical city of Ur. In 1922 Sir Leonard Woolley, a British archaeologist, began extensive digging at the site. In *Mesopotamia,* the land between the Tigris and Euphrates Rivers (in modern Iraq), Woolley uncovered many treasures from Ur and the land it belonged to, called Sumer.

These writings and objects, long hidden under the sand, tell us about the Sumerians, whose kingdoms lasted one thousand years. We know, for instance, that Ur, like other Sumerian cities, was a grand place surrounded by high walls and boasting huge palaces and plazas. People of Abraham's day used canals to irrigate their fields; they grew grain and vegetables and sold wool to other countries. They were weavers and metalworkers; they studied medicine and the stars.

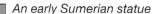

An early Sumerian statue

The Metropolitan Museum of Art, Harris Brisbane Dick Fund, 1959 (59.2) Photograph©1981 The Metropolitan Museum of Art

Inscription on a brick in the ruins of Ur

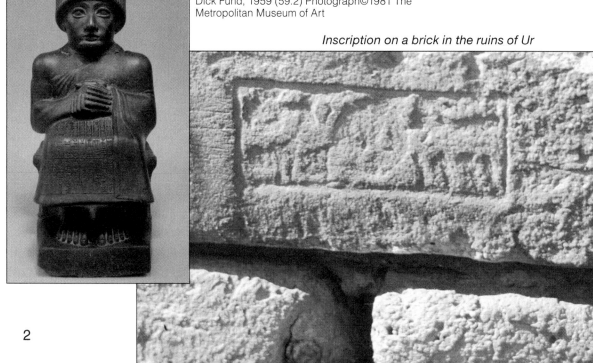

Mesopotamia

Location—Modern Iraq contains much of what we recognize as ancient Mesopotamia. It is located in the Middle East at the head of the Persian Gulf. Kuwait and Saudi Arabia form its southern border. Jordan and Syria on the west, Turkey on the north, and Iran on the east make up its other borders.

Climate—Iraq receives an average of seven inches of rainfall per year. Temperatures range from 50°F in the winter to 93°F in the summer.

Topography—Lower Iraq is a low floodplain between the southern Tigris and Euphrates Rivers. Upper Iraq has rolling hills and fertile soil. Mountains rise in the northeast, and the west is desert.

Natural Resources—Petroleum and some natural gas. The Tigris and Euphrates Rivers provide water for irrigation.

Geography and Culture—The rivers of Mesopotamia provided an ideal place for civilization to flourish. The Tigris and Euphrates watered the land for farming. They also provided fish for food and a highway for transportation and communication.

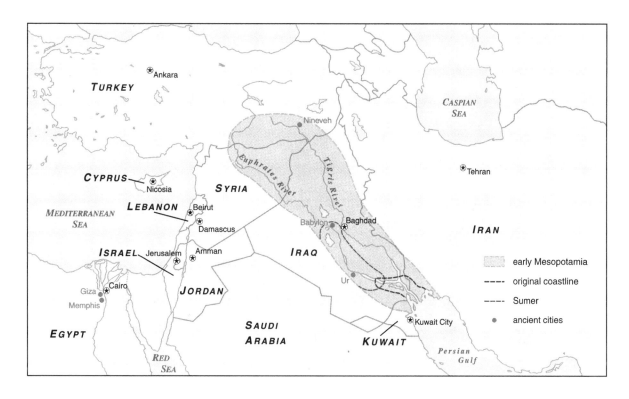

3

How We Find Out About the Past

Look at the pictures on this page. What do you think they look like? Like a chicken left its footprints in wet clay? Although those marks may look like hen scratchings, they are really words written nearly five thousand years ago in Sumer.

Such writings have often puzzled *archaeologists,* men and women who study objects from the past to learn about the people who made and used them. Manmade objects, called *artifacts*—such as clay tablets, pottery, jewelry, sculptures, and coins—often give clues about a person's lifestyle or character traits. A woman's jewelry could reveal whether she was rich and powerful or poor but inventive.

Archaeologists usually find artifacts by digging. An archaeological *dig* or excavation may be small or large. Every dig needs experts in photography, architecture, translation, and drawing to interpret and preserve what is found. Archaeologists sometimes choose an excavation site by the presence of a *tell,* or mound. *Tell* comes from the Arabic word for "high" and refers to a hill built up over the centuries. Such mounds result from drifting sand settling in layers over cities that have been destroyed and rebuilt time and again.

Sumerian writing on a relief carving (left), small tablets (right), and a drum-shaped document (below)

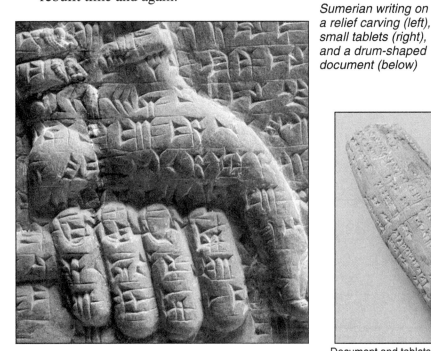

Document and tablets, Bob Jones University Bible Lands Museum

4

Tags mark the locations of artifacts found at this archaeological dig.

Work on the tell begins with air and ground surveys. From this information the archaeologists draw a map and section off the area into squares. Today archaeologists often use computers to help keep records and make calculations. The actual digging is done slowly, a layer at a time. Everyone must work carefully to avoid damaging fragile objects. When an object is found, it is photographed, recorded, and tagged.

The clues and information, thus patiently uncovered, are the source for much of what you will read in this book. You will not have to decipher ancient writing, but you may be asked to draw conclusions about the people of the past.

5

Archaeology and the Old Testament

Because they reject the Bible and a worldwide flood, many secular archaeologists and historians assume that Sumer was one of the first civilizations. Although there are no written records or other artifacts from before the Flood, we know that the earlier civilizations were quite advanced. Genesis 4 says that the people before Noah built cities, were skilled musicians and workers in brass and iron, and knew much about agriculture. The fact that we have no physical evidence of pre-Flood civilization is no reason to doubt the Bible.

Other assumptions researchers have made about the events in the Bible have been proved wrong in many archaeological sites. For example, some people used to reject the story of Abraham as a myth because they assumed that camels, such as the one Rebekah rode to meet Isaac, would not have been used as beasts of burden in Abraham's time. But Sumerian tablets not only record that indeed camels were ridden then but also tell how: behind the hump.

Furthermore, discoveries of skeletons in caves around Ur explain the Bible phrase "gathered to his people." The same burial caves were used by Sumerians for generations. Thus, Abraham's sons were following a common custom when they buried him.

Sumer of Mesopotamia

The land around Ur has changed little since Abraham's day. It is still dry and dusty, the clay soil often made hard by the sun. The Tigris and Euphrates Rivers still wind their way slowly through the flat plains, and the people practice many of the same skills and professions as their ancestors.

Farmers and Fishermen

Outside the great city of Ur, farmers worked hard in their fields. Irrigation canals crisscrossed the fields, bringing water from the river to the soil. Mesopotamia had few natural resources, but the Sumerians made good use of the crucial natural resource of water. Modern farmers also use irrigation to grow crops in places too dry for agriculture.

Sumerian farmers may have been the first people to use the wheel. You can imagine that pulling a heavy load on a cart with wheels was much easier than dragging that same load along on a skid. Sumerian farmers also used plows pulled by oxen. The oxen were hitched to the plow with a yoke, another implement first recorded in Sumer. The yoke helped the oxen to pull a plow or a heavy wagonload.

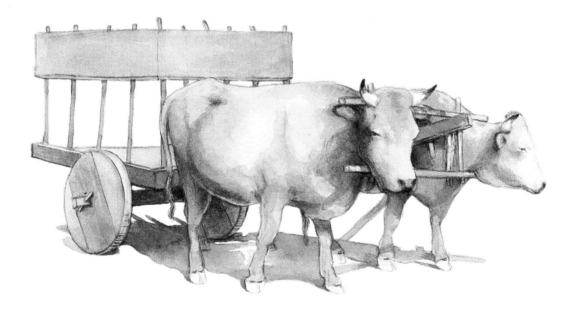

The farmers of Sumer grew nearly all that the people needed: barley, wheat, peas, onions, garlic, leeks, lettuce, turnips, cucumbers, sesame seeds, dates, and figs. The farmers who owned their own land sold their harvests in the city market. Many farmers did not own their own land but worked on land owned by the temple or by wealthy individuals. They received part of the harvest to use or sell.

Fibers of flax (above) and wool shorn from sheep (below) were used in Sumerian clothing.

A very important crop in Sumer was *flax*. The Sumerians spun linen thread from the long fibers of the flax plant and then wove those fibers into cloth.

The farmers also raised animals, such as donkeys and oxen, to work in the fields and transport heavy loads. Goats, pigs, and sheep supplied meat as well as hides and wool. Sheep were so important to the Sumerians that they had over two hundred different words to describe all the breeds.

On the Euphrates, which ran along the eastern side of Ur, sailed many boats. Some were trading ships that had come from faraway places. Many, however, were fishing boats owned by local fishermen. Every day the fishermen went to the river and then returned home to sell their catches at the city market. Fish and bread were the most important foods of the Sumerians' diet.

Merchants and Traders

At the edge of the city, on the Euphrates River, stood the docks where trading ships and fishing boats anchored. Dockworkers, merchants, traders, and sailors carried on their business there. Ships brought goods from as far away as India in the east and Egypt in the west. Their holds were loaded with stone, wood, gems, and metals—goods for the workshops of Ur. Why do you think Sumer imported these goods? It had none of them as natural resources.

The Sumerians kept careful records of all their business dealings. *Scribes* wrote down every sale with a reed *stylus* on a tablet made of soft clay. The writing, one of the greatest accomplishments of Sumer, is called *cuneiform* from the Latin words for "wedge-shaped." The Sumerian language had over six hundred symbols that stood for words, numbers, or syllables. After a scribe recorded a transaction, he wrapped the tablet in another piece of clay that served as an envelope. When the tablet dried, it was stored in the temple with other legal records. From these careful records we have learned much about Sumerian economics.

When two merchants finished a business deal and the scribe put his last marks on the tablet, each man had to sign it. They did not use the scribe's stylus to write their names. Rather they used clay seals shaped like cylinders. The *cylinder seal* was small, only about one to two inches high and about a half-inch in diameter. It had carvings that identified the owner. The carvings included plants, animals, gods, and wedge-shaped symbols. Each man rolled his seal across the wet clay tablet to approve the sale. The cylinder seal was a fast, simple way to sign one's name. The mark of a cylinder seal stood either for approval, as on a legal document, or for ownership, as on goods ready to be shipped.

"He that hath received his testimony hath set to his seal that God is true."

John 3:33

Cylinder seals (right) and impressions from seals (above), Bob Jones University Bible Lands Museum

To Make a Cylinder Seal

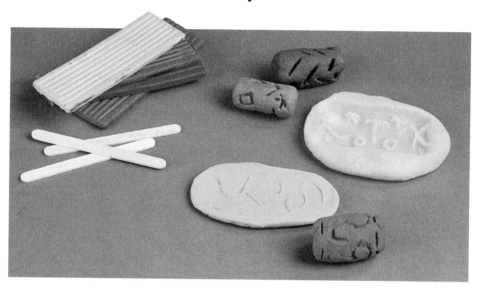

1. Decide what design would best represent you on the seal.

2. Get the clay and styling tool from your teacher. Shape the clay into a cylinder about two inches long and one inch wide. With your styling tool, create your signature picture or design around the clay cylinder. Let the clay harden.

3. On another day make small tablets with the remaining clay. Roll your cylinder seal over a clay tablet to imprint your signature.

Artisans and Buyers

Unloaded goods did not stay long at the docks. Workers gathered them up and took them into the city. In the center of Ur, skilled craftsmen, also called *artisans,* turned raw materials into finished goods. These products made up most of Sumer's *exports,* goods sold to foreign traders. Archaeologists have found both records and remains of jewelry, pottery, clothing, and other objects fashioned in the artisans' shops.

Many of the workshops in Ur produced goods for everyday use. Some of the busiest shops in the city were those that sold cloth. The cloth makers employed many women to spin thread from flax or wool and then weave it into cloth. The people of Ur bought their cloth at one shop, had it dyed at another, and then took it home to make clothing.

After leaving the cloth maker's shop, a shopper might have stopped at a pottery workshop. Clay was one of the few raw materials plentiful in the river valley. While the potters busily threw clay onto their wheels and formed pots, the shopper ordered his goods. Sumerians were possibly the first to use a potter's wheel to make clay pots. Before that time, pots had to be molded or coiled by hand, but the wheel allowed a potter to produce pots of uniform size and shape faster than before. Potters in Ur made all sorts of containers for storing and serving food. The potters added carvings and decorations to make the pots attractive as well as useful.

Potters still work at their wheels. The potters' wheels have changed little over the centuries. The potters' designs of pitchers, bowls, cups, and plates are also much the same. But now tourists can buy this beautiful pottery as souvenirs, and huge ships can carry these lovely works of art to countries that had not been imagined when Abraham left Ur.

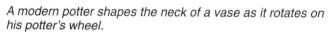

A modern potter shapes the neck of a vase as it rotates on his potter's wheel.

Pottery on the docks in modern Kuwait

13

The Standard of Ur, *Sumerian art made of shell inlay with red limestone and lapis lazuli set in bitumen on a wooden case*

The city also had shops that made luxury goods. The artisans of these shops trained for many years to learn the skills for making beautiful objects. Several workshops made jewelry and fine dishes from the gold, silver, copper, and precious jewels imported into Sumer. The finished pieces, intricately and beautifully designed, were either sold in Ur or shipped to other lands.

A special craft in Ur was *shell inlay*. An artisan used white shells from the river and arranged them into a design. He had to make sure the pieces fit together well, almost like pieces of a puzzle. Once satisfied with his design, he pressed the pieces into softened tar on another surface, such as metal. After the main design was finished, he may have surrounded it with a bright blue stone called *lapis lazuli*. A shell inlay artisan had to be patient and careful. Some works of sparkling white shells and lapis lazuli inlay still exist and show us the high quality of Sumerian workmanship.

Priests and Worshipers

In the center of Ur, both four thousand years ago and today, stands the temple tower, called a *ziggurat*. The ziggurat and surrounding temple buildings took up about one-fourth of the city. People approaching the city could see the ziggurat while they were still a long distance away. It rose in three levels with gardens planted on each terrace and with a shrine on the top. An area beside the ziggurat formed a temple complex, complete with a few other large structures containing shrines, homes for the high priestess and many temple workers, a storehouse, and additional chambers.

The Sumerians were polytheistic in their worship. The word *polytheism* comes from the Greek words meaning "many gods." The gods the Sumerians worshiped were false gods made up by men and acting like men.

View looking up the steps of the ziggurat

The reconstructed ziggurat in Ur

Each Sumerian city had one god in particular whom the people worshiped. In Ur the people worshiped the moon god *Nanna.* They believed that the god lived in the ziggurat, in a little shrine at the very top. His statue was kept there and food was offered to him daily. The priests and priestesses who lived at the temple used these offerings to perform magic rituals or to meet their own needs. The priests held powerful positions in Sumer because the Sumerians believed that the priests had more power with the gods than did the common people.

The Sumerians did not believe that their city-god cared about their everyday problems. They thought that he had larger concerns dealing with other gods and earthly kings. Instead, they trusted lesser gods whose statues they worshiped at home. They thought that these gods acted as go-betweens to gods of greater power.

The Sumerians worshiped their gods by praying to them, giving them gifts, and performing rituals. They believed that if the gods were pleased, the people would prosper. If the gods were not pleased, disaster would strike. Religious rituals and prayers accompanied all the Sumerians' activities, no matter how ordinary.

Stone statue from Tell Asmar, Iraq. (detail) Early dynastic (Sumerian), 2600 B.C

Iraq Museum, Baghdad, Iraq

Kings and Subjects

The temple was important not only as the center of religion but also as the seat of the Sumerian government. Sumer was made up of several city-states. A *city-state* is an independent city and its surrounding land. The Sumerian city-states often fought against each other, with kings trying to gain more land and power from the other city-states. During Abraham's lifetime, Ur was the most powerful Sumerian city-state.

Every city-state had its own king and its own god. The king was the god's highest representative on earth. The people looked on him as a god too. He lived in a lavish palace within the temple complex, and he ruled from his throne. Slaves and other servants waited upon him; court musicians played instruments and sang his praises.

Whatever the kings demanded, citizens did. Some kings wrote down laws and ruled by them. In Ur a lawbreaker often had to pay fines as punishment. For example, if a man cut off another man's foot or nose, he paid the injured man a certain amount of silver. Legal records were required on all business transactions, contracts, marriages, adoptions, and wills. Archaeologists have found many of Sumer's records, still in their clay envelopes, filed in the temple.

Ruins of the palace/temple complex in Ur

School-fathers and Students

Near the ziggurat in Ur was a large house with an unusual guest room and courtyard. This building puzzled archaeologists for a while until they realized it was the home of a scribe who operated a school. (The chief clue was two thousand clay tablets found in the building.)

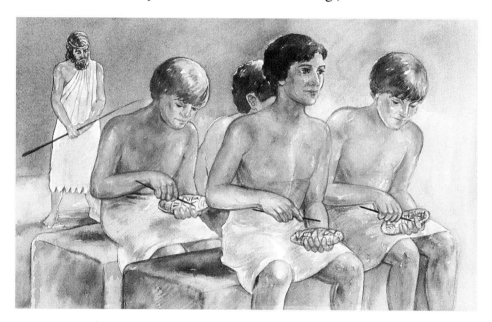

Usually only boys from wealthy families were able to attend school in Ur. The instruction helped them learn to become good scribes. Students who learned to write well became highly respected in Sumer. They practiced making the wedge-shaped symbols of Sumerian writing during the long school days, with only six free days each month. To help the students discipline themselves to study, the school had a teacher called "the man in charge of the whip."

The Sumerians called the school building the *tablet-house*. All day the *school-father*, or chief teacher, gave students lessons to practice. They wrote lists, did mathematical problems, and learned grammar. An assistant, called a "big brother," wrote out assignments for the young students to copy and then checked their work. To practice reading, the students recited their tablets aloud both at school and home.

Making Up Proverbs

"Into an open mouth, a fly enters."

This was a saying many schoolboys often heard. The Sumerians liked *proverbs,* or wise sayings. Proverbs give bits of wisdom in a short, easy-to-remember form. Sometimes Sumerian proverbs expressed a simple truth: "A sweet word is everybody's friend." Other proverbs showed a contrast between two types of behavior: "A loving heart builds the home; a hating heart destroys the home." Some offered commonsense observations on life: "A scribe whose hand moves as fast as the mouth, that's a scribe for you."

19

Parents and Children

Ur was a bustling city of perhaps fifty thousand people. Simple houses crowded the narrow, winding streets and alleys. Most of these houses had only one outside door and no windows. The thick mud walls kept the houses cool in the hot Mesopotamian climate.

Wealthy families lived in two-story houses. Each house had a large central courtyard, off which smaller rooms for cooking, sleeping, and entertaining opened. There was a special room for the family's statue of their personal god. The furniture was a few low tables and perhaps some chairs and a bed. Woolen and reed mats lined the walls and floors. Often the family slept and entertained guests outdoors on the flat roof, where the air was cooler in the evenings.

The families in Ur were small for ancient times. Most families had four or five children. Girls stayed at home and learned housekeeping skills from their mothers. Boys learned trades or skills from their fathers or went to school. When children reached marrying age, the parents arranged the marriages for them. They tried to choose a hard-working partner for each child.

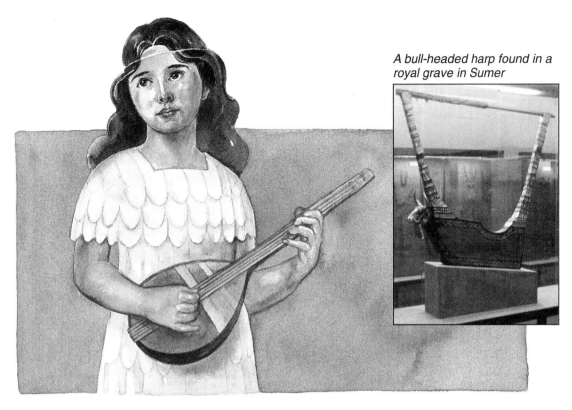

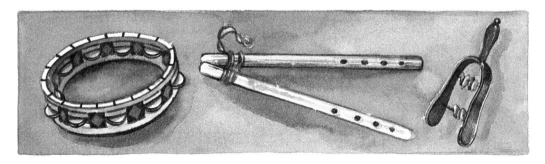

A bull-headed harp found in a royal grave in Sumer

Parents encouraged their children to work and to study hard. In the evenings fathers listened to their sons recite their daily lessons. Families also spent the evenings singing and playing musical instruments, such as harps, lyres, drums, tambourines, and pipes (instruments similar to flutes). Music was important to religious rituals and daily work as well.

Parents in Sumer believed in strong discipline. They taught their children obedience and respect. A child who disobeyed might even be disowned or disinherited by his father. The values of hard work and discipline instilled in these Sumerian children helped them to become industrious adults and to maintain an impressive civilization.

Numbering the Years

Nearly fifteen hundred years ago people stopped using the old system of numbering years from the founding of Rome. Instead they decided to number years from the birth of Jesus Christ.

Scholars decided that if events were earlier than Christ's birth, the year would be labeled B.C. (*before Christ.*) If they were after Christ's birth, the year would be labeled A.D. (short for *anno Domini,* the Latin words for "in the year of the Lord").

Usually we do not use the letters A.D. unless we think there will be some confusion. For example, if someone lived from 43 B.C. until A.D. 25, we include the letters to show that he lived sixty-eight years rather than eighteen.

Every time someone writes a date—whether referring to Sumer in 2500 B.C. or an event last year in New York City—he is really "echoing" the most important event in human history.

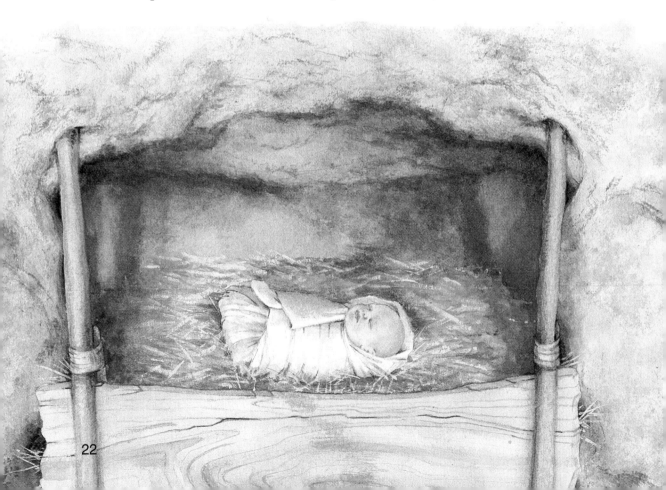

2

The Gift of the Nile:
Ancient Egypt

Rami lowered the *shadoof* one last time. That should be enough water, he thought. I'm so tired! He stretched his arms over his head to ease his cramped muscles and nearly tumbled over backward. He looked out over his family's fields. The grain was almost ready to harvest. It waved in the hot winds blowing in from the desert.

Rami smiled. He was glad he had the important job of keeping his father's irrigation canals full of water. Without the water of the Nile, no crops could grow. Without those crops, he would not have a lunch to eat.

Soon the men from the village would cut the grain. Rami would help again this year by tying the sheaves of grain into bundles. After harvest, the villagers would spread the bundles of grain on the threshing floor and drive the farm animals over them. The trampling hooves would shake the ripe grain from the stalks, and then each family would store its grain in a silo for the next year's bread.

Rami sat down and leaned against a large palm tree. "It won't be long," he said aloud, "and there will be feasting and giving thanks to the gods for such a good harvest." He stretched and yawned. "Then all we'll have to do is wait for the season of flooding."

Ancient Egypt and the Nile

Egypt has been called "The Gift of the Nile." Why do you think Egypt was given this name? Without the Nile River, it would not have existed. The great civilization that lasted for more than three thousand years would not have developed. The great pyramids, the Sphinx, and the temples of Egypt would not have been built.

No one knows just when the Egyptians settled along the Nile River. They may have arrived as early as thirty-eight hundred years before the birth of Christ. Imagine how these early travelers to Egypt felt after their long trip. Suddenly, right in front of them flowed a mighty river. What do you think these people thought about the river?

All Egyptians throughout history honored and gave thanks to the Nile. They gave it the nickname *Hapi*, which means "well-fed" or "fat." They worshiped the Nile as a god. The following lines are from the "Hymn to the Nile":

Hail to thee, O Nile, that issues from the earth and comes to keep Egypt alive! . . . The bringer of food, rich in provision, creator of all good, lord of majesty, sweet of fragrance.

If you were to fly over Egypt and look out the window of the airplane, you would see desert in all directions. This is the great Sahara, a desert that covers most of North Africa. Soon you would see a thin ribbon of green cutting the desert into two parts. In the middle of that green ribbon would be a silver thread, the mighty Nile River.

The early settlers in Egypt soon discovered that wherever the Nile River flowed, plants grew. Where there was no water, all was desert. At the edge of Egyptian farms like Rami's, a person could stand with one foot in green grass and the other foot in yellow desert sand.

Egypt

Location—Northeastern Africa. Ancient Egypt was the land along the Nile River; modern Egypt is a square of territory bounded by Libya, Sudan, the Red Sea, and the Mediterranean Sea.

Climate—Mostly dry, except for the area along the banks of the Nile. Temperatures range from 107°F in the summer to 55°F in the winter.

Topography—Dominated by the Nile River and its valley; desert to the east and west of the Nile; Sinai Peninsula in eastern Egypt.

Natural Resources—Granite, iron ore, petroleum, and date palms. Its greatest resource is the water brought by the Nile.

Geography and Culture—Life in Egypt was sustained by the Nile because of its provisions for farming, hunting, trade, transportation, and political unity.

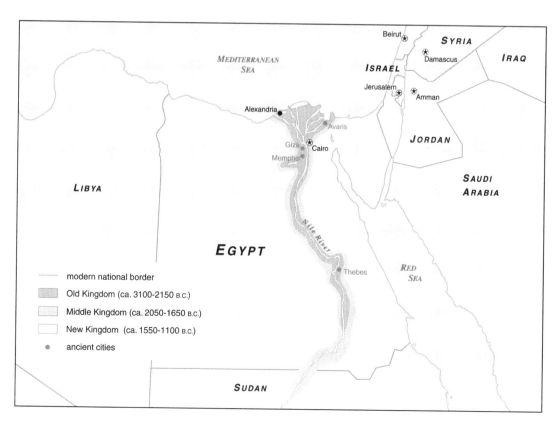

- modern national border
- Old Kingdom (ca. 3100-2150 B.C.)
- Middle Kingdom (ca. 2050-1650 B.C.)
- New Kingdom (ca. 1550-1100 B.C.)
- • ancient cities

Each summer in ancient Egypt, the Nile overflowed its banks. Melting snows in African mountains and heavy spring rains far to the south caused the river to rise dramatically. The water rushed down the mountains and across the flat land of Egypt. Soon everything except the tallest palm trees was under water. The flood lasted for four months. During that time, the water soaked into the land. It also deposited a layer of rich soil on top of the land.

When the land was nearly dry, Egyptian farmers like Rami's father went into their fields. They did not have to plow but simply scattered their seeds onto the damp ground. After that, they walked the farm animals back and forth across the field. The animals' hooves pushed the seeds into the soil.

All that families had to do after that was to water the crops. Remember the shadoof that Rami used? It is a long pole with a weight on one end and a bucket on the other. Rami dipped the bucket into the Nile River, pulled it up, and emptied it into the irrigation canals. It was hard work and had to be done every day until the crops were ready to harvest. If a family had a donkey or an ox, they could use it to turn a water wheel to raise water to the fields. But few could afford such luxuries.

cucumbers

Egyptians who lived long before Rami's time built irrigation canals so that they could plant more crops. The strip of fertile land along the Nile River was only about ten miles wide. But it stretched the whole length of the river.

At the north end of the Nile, where it flows into the Mediterranean Sea, the early settlers found a much larger area to farm. The waters of the Nile separated into many smaller rivers and flowed out into a fan shape. This fan shape is called a *delta*. It looks a bit like a flower on a long stem. Egyptians who settled here did not have to worry about water because the land was low and swampy. They grew cucumbers, melons, and date palms.

When everything went well, the people ate very well. They had wheat and barley, melons and cucumbers, onions and garlic, dates and figs. The river supplied them with many kinds of fish and waterfowl. They also raised animals for meat.

garlic

figs

pomegranate

onions

dates

29

Egypt was the storehouse of the ancient world. Large harvests allowed Egyptians to store food for times of famine when the Nile River did not rise to soak the land and leave its rich soil behind. Because of their careful planning, the Egyptians usually had more than enough to eat.

Foreigners knew of Egypt's bounty, and many traveled there when in need. As you will soon see, God used Egypt as a temporary place of safety and prosperity for His chosen people.

In this Egyptian wall painting, the colorfully-clad people in the middle band may be Hebrews being presented to the pharaoh.

All of Egypt depended on the Nile River. Government officials kept detailed records of when the river flooded and how high the water rose. They used a device called a *nilometer.* From these measurements, they calculated the taxes the people owed. Egyptians paid taxes according to how good their crops were, and those crops depended on the waters of the Nile.

Because of the importance of the Nile floods, the priests developed a calendar that would tell them the exact days that the Nile was supposed to flood. This calendar had only three seasons: Flood (Akhit), Planting (Perit), and Harvest (Shemu).

Old Kingdom (ca. 3100-2150 B.C.)

In the first centuries after the early settlers came, Egypt was divided into two kingdoms. The area around the Nile delta was called the Lower Kingdom, and the area along the rest of the river was the Upper Kingdom.

About the year 3100 B.C., the ruler of the city Hierankonopolis conquered all of the villages and cities along the Nile River. His name was Narmer. Do you think this sounds like a royal name? It really means "catfish." Narmer was the first king, or pharaoh, of a united Egypt. Historians call this the Old Kingdom of Egypt. Although Egypt was one kingdom, people still recognized Lower and Upper Egypt as two separate geographical regions.

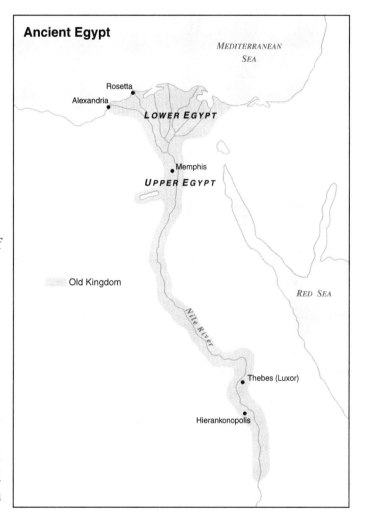

Ancient Egypt

MEDITERRANEAN SEA

Rosetta

Alexandria

LOWER EGYPT

Memphis

UPPER EGYPT

Old Kingdom

RED SEA

Nile River

Thebes (Luxor)

Hierankonopolis

Making Mummies and Pyramids

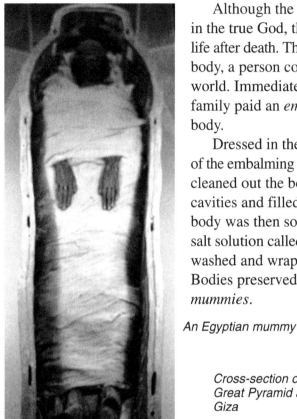

Although the Egyptians did not believe in the true God, they were firm believers in life after death. They believed that without a body, a person could not exist in the next world. Immediately after a person died, his family paid an *embalmer* to preserve his body.

Dressed in the jackal-headed costume of the embalming god, Anubis, the embalmer cleaned out the body's skull and abdominal cavities and filled them with spices. The body was then soaked for seventy days in a salt solution called *natron*. Afterward, it was washed and wrapped in linen bandages. Bodies preserved in this way were called *mummies*.

An Egyptian mummy

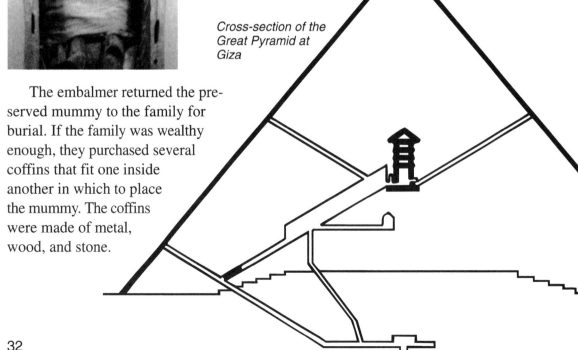

Cross-section of the Great Pyramid at Giza

The embalmer returned the preserved mummy to the family for burial. If the family was wealthy enough, they purchased several coffins that fit one inside another in which to place the mummy. The coffins were made of metal, wood, and stone.

The Egyptian pharaoh was a man of great power. During the Old Kingdom, Egyptians began to believe that the pharaoh was a god. Pharaohs had large burial chambers built and filled with food, clothing, furniture, and even games and toys. The pharaohs thought that they would need these things to bring them pleasure and ease in the next life. They thought that small statues of gods placed in the tombs would act as servants and that scenes of daily life painted on the walls would make them feel at home. All other Egyptians who could afford to do so followed this practice.

The most famous of these tombs are Khufu's three pyramids at Giza. Khufu had the largest of these pyramids, the Great Pyramid, built around 2500 B.C. It covers 13 acres and measures about 756 feet on each side. The house you live in would fit inside it, along with several of your neighbors' houses.

Khufu also ordered the building of the Sphinx, a large stone statue near the pyramids. He is said to have seen a huge rock while working on his pyramid and thought that it looked like a lion lying in the desert. He had his workers finish the sculpture and make the lion's head look like him.

The Sphinx and the Great Pyramid at Giza

The pharaohs built other things besides pyramids. In the cities of Memphis and Thebes, they constructed beautiful palaces, storehouses, and many temples to their gods. The pharaohs' slaves dug irrigation canals for the farmers along the Nile so that new fields could be planted. The canals also helped control the floodwaters of the Nile.

Much of our information about the Old Kingdom comes from artifacts left behind by the Egyptians. The largest artifacts are the great pyramids and the Sphinx. The colorful paintings inside the pyramids tell us a great deal about the daily life of Egyptians in the Old Kingdom. What other artifacts might have been left behind by these early Egyptians?

Papyrus is the most important artifact. It is a paper made from the stalk of the papyrus plant, a reed that grows along the banks of the Nile. This paper was light and thin and could be stored easily. The Egyptians used it for thousands of years to keep records, write letters, and tell stories. When the apostle Paul dictated his letter to the Romans, his scribe, Tertius, probably wrote on a scroll of papyrus. People of Europe continued using papyrus until the Middle Ages.

Papyrus being harvested along the Nile

To make paper, early Egyptians cut papyrus stems into sections which they peeled and sliced. These slices were soaked, layered, covered, and pounded. The finished paper was then dried before use.

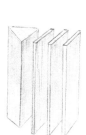

The Rosetta Stone

Egyptian writing is called *hieroglyphics,* or picture writing. People drew pictures of the ideas they wanted to express. This kind of writing was used from 3100 B.C. to A.D. 1100—longer than any other kind in the world.

For many centuries after the Egyptian civilization declined, no one could read hieroglyphs. In 1799, a large, black stone was found in the sand of the Nile delta. The message carved on the stone was written in two important languages. One of them was Egyptian hieroglyphs. The other was Greek, a language read by many educated Europeans.

The Rosetta stone

Have you ever tried to decipher a coded message? To break the code, you have to compare it to a language that is familiar to you. A Frenchman named Jean Champollion worked many years to decipher the hieroglyphs by comparing them with the Greek. Finally, in 1822, he succeeded. People interested in Egypt could now read letters and books over four thousand years old.

Modern restorers at work repairing and preserving hieroglyphics in the tomb of Queen Nefertari, wife of Rameses II

35

To Draw and Read Hieroglyphics

1. Working with your team, make up a hieroglyphic alphabet, substituting a picture for each letter of the English alphabet.

2. Write a short message using your hieroglyphs.

3. Choose three words in the message and write the English translation below them.

4. Exchange your message with another team and try to decode each other's message.

The Old Kingdom lasted for over nine hundred years. The last weak pharaohs could not make the princes obey them. The princes actually fought each other to win more land and power. After more than a century of fighting, one of the princes was able to unite Egypt again.

This Egyptian makeup kit was used during the Middle Kingdom.

Middle Kingdom (ca. 2050-1650 B.C.)

Pharaoh Amenemnes of Thebes was not a great warrior, but he was a good politician. He reunited Egypt and set up a new government. He built a wall to protect his people from invasion. Trade flourished up and down the Nile, and the army conquered part of the Sudan.

The pharaohs of the Middle Kingdom built temples, small pyramids, and forts. Like the pharoahs before them, they decorated their palaces and tombs with sculptures and paintings.

Joseph (Genesis 37-50)

Sold to merchants by his jealous brothers, Joseph was taken to Egypt around 1897 B.C., during the reign of Sesostris II. He was bought as a slave by Potiphar, the captain of the pharaoh's guard.

Joseph had already made up his mind that, no matter where he was, he would serve God. Potiphar soon trusted his new slave with all he owned. One day Potiphar's wife told a lie about Joseph because she wanted to get even with him. Potiphar believed his wife and put Joseph into prison.

But even there, God blessed Joseph for his faithfulness. When the keeper of the prison discovered that he could trust Joseph, he put him in charge of the prison. During this time, Pharaoh Sesostris II learned that Joseph could interpret dreams, and he told him his dream of starving cows and withered ears of corn. Joseph explained to the pharaoh that this dream

was God's message about a famine that would last for seven years but that Sesostris II would have seven years of good harvests to save food and prepare.

How do you think Sesostris felt about Joseph now? Sesostris was so grateful to be able to understand his dream that he gave Joseph his royal ring and made him the *vizier,* or the second highest official in government. Joseph saved one-fifth of all the crops for the next seven years to prepare for the famine. He also collected taxes and served as Egypt's chief judge.

When the famine years came, the Egyptians went to Joseph to buy food. He opened the storehouses. There was enough for everyone. In Canaan, Jacob's family also suffered from the famine. He sent his sons to Egypt to purchase food.

When Joseph saw the strangers from Canaan, he recognized his brothers. He forgave them and gave them food. Soon after, Jacob moved his family to Egypt. They settled in the land of Goshen near the Nile delta.

The last years of the Middle Kingdom were not peaceful. The pharaohs were more interested in riches than in ruling. They did not strengthen the borders of Egypt or keep the walls repaired. A people called the *Hyksos* invaded Egypt. They attacked the cities and countryside and took whatever they wanted. The Egyptian army could not stop them because the Hyksos had a new weapon: the horse-drawn chariot.

In 1630 B.C., the Hyksos conquered Egypt and made Avaris their capital city. They tried to live and rule like the pharaohs. They even worshiped Egyptian gods. They dressed in Egyptian clothes, lived in Egyptian houses, and ate Egyptian food.

The Hebrews, the descendants of Joseph and his brothers, held important positions in Egypt at this time. The Hyksos feared that the Hebrews might become

A North African man using a brick-making process similar to that used by Hebrew slaves in ancient Egypt

powerful enough to take over the government. To keep this from happening, the Hyksos forced the Hebrews into slavery. They made the Hebrews farm their fields, build cities for them, and make all the bricks for the buildings.

Finally, Ahmose, an Egyptian prince of Thebes, raised an army. He attacked the Hyksos, captured their capital city, and drove them out of the land. Egypt was once again united, but Ahmose did not free the Hebrews.

An Egyptian-style illustration of slaves making bricks

New Kingdom (ca. 1550-1100 B.C.)

In 1550 B.C., Ahmose became the first pharaoh of the New Kingdom. He and his successors made Egypt mightier than it had ever been. They used the horse-drawn chariot to invade Palestine and Syria. Egypt's empire soon stretched all the way to the upper Euphrates River. The people of southern Egypt traded with the Sudan for gold and ivory. It was the greatest period of Egyptian history, but the Egyptians kept the Hebrew people enslaved.

It was during the New Kingdom, probably under Amenhotep II's reign, that God raised up Moses to free His chosen people from slavery in Egypt. Moses, a Hebrew child, was given the privilege of being brought up in the pharaoh's household. He learned to read and write and studied history, arithmetic, and science. As an adult, Moses left Egypt and became a shepherd in Midian.

From a burning bush in the desert, the Lord called Moses to return to Egypt and lead the Hebrews to freedom. Moses went before Amenhotep II to ask him to free the slaves. When Amenhotep refused, God sent a series of ten plagues on the Egyptians. After the last plague, when all the first-born sons of the Egyptians were dead, Amenhotep finally agreed to let the Hebrews go.

A few days later, after the Hebrews had left, Amenhotep changed his mind again. He chased the Hebrews with six hundred chariots and an army of men, but the Lord protected His chosen ones. He destroyed all of Amenhotep's army in the waters of the Red Sea.

Tutankhamen (ca. 1358-1339 B.C.)

Would you like to be the ruler of a kingdom at the age you are now? What kinds of decisions would you have to make? Whom would you consult for advice?

Tutankhamen was only about ten years old when he became pharaoh of Egypt. He died when he was only nineteen. He did not do anything of importance during his short reign. The world would not have paid him any attention at all, except that his tomb was discovered intact on November 4, 1922, by British archaeologist Howard Carter.

Inside King Tut's tomb, Carter found wonderful treasure. It took him over eight years to catalog all the statues, furniture, toys, pottery, and precious objects he found. Because King Tut's tomb was found, we now know a great deal about how the pharaohs lived and died.

Rameses II was one of the last pharaohs who kept the empire strong. He defeated the Hittites, a warrior people from Asia Minor. He also built some of the greatest temples in Egypt. Karnak is the most famous. Rameses also had many colossal statues made of himself.

Statue of Rameses II

Colossal statues of Rameses II guarding the Abu Simbel temple (below), with a closeup view of one of the statues (left)

Rameses II deserves to be called great. He was a great warrior. He worked hard at being a wise and good pharaoh, and he was kind to his subjects. When he died, he was buried in a beautiful tomb. Although this tomb was broken into by grave robbers, Rameses II's mummy was not destroyed. Today it is in the Cairo Museum.

After the death of Rameses II around 1213 B.C., Egypt grew weaker. The pharaohs were not able to protect the empire from invaders. Barely two hundred years after Rameses's death, people from the west invaded Egypt. From then on, Egyptians were ruled by foreigners until the twentieth century, when the modern state of Egypt was formed.

Religion in Ancient Egypt

Although the people of Egypt had seen the power of the one true God, they refused to believe in Him. They continued to worship their own false gods. Egypt had hundreds of gods—one for each village and city. Families built altars in their houses to worship their favorite gods. The worship of many gods is called *polytheism.*

Anubis

Isis

Horus

Osiris

All Egyptians believed that Ra, the sun god, created and ruled the world. During the Middle Kingdom, the priests of Thebes joined their god, Amon, to Ra. They called the new god Amon-Ra. The priests then had to tell everyone how to worship the new god. This made them very powerful.

Osiris, the god of the underworld, was a favorite of the Egyptians. They believed that after burial, a dead person traveled by boat to the Hall of Judgment, where Osiris presided. Anubis, the jackal-headed god, weighed the dead person's heart against the feather of justice, order, and truth. During judgment, the dead person quoted from the *Book of the Dead,* saying, "I have not committed evil against men. . . . I have not taken milk from the mouths of children. . . . I have not mistreated cattle," and "I am pure!" What do you think about this belief?

Osiris's wife, Isis, protected children. Horus, their son, had the body of a man and the head of a falcon or a hawk. These three gods formed the model family that Egyptians tried to follow. There were gods of medicine, education, music, and even love. Hathor, the goddess of love, had the body of a woman and the head of a cow.

Egyptians believed that the pharoah was the son of Horus. This made the pharaoh a god and the high priest of Egypt. Every morning, after washing and dressing, the pharaoh went to the temple to "awaken" the idol of Horus. He washed and clothed the idol, gave it food, and put makeup on it. Now, everyone believed, the day could proceed with the god's blessing.

Only one pharaoh tried to change the religion of Egypt. His name was Amenhotep IV (1356-1340 B.C.). He believed there was only one great god, Aton. The pharaoh even changed his name to Akhenaton to show that he worshiped the god Aton.

How do you think the people felt about this change? The priests of the old gods did not like losing their influence. The Egyptians did not want to give up the old gods either. Akhenaton was murdered, and his successor, Tutankhamen, returned to the old religion.

An Egyptian relief carving showing Akhenaton and his wife with the sun god Aton

Culture in Ancient Egypt

The ancient Egyptians loved music. It was part of everyday life, not just for celebrations. They sang praises to the Nile. They sang while they worked in the fields. Children sang while they played. Craftsmen and traders sang as they worked in their shops or sailed up and down the Nile. Slaves made their chores less tedious by singing. Religious ceremonies used many songs, both of praise and of prayer to the gods. The pharaoh and nobles often had musicians to entertain them.

Egyptians were known for their cleanliness. They wore fresh clothing of linen, cotton, or wool. Both men and women used cosmetics and wore wigs made from human hair and beeswax. Women usually wore their hair long, while men were bald or cropped their hair just above their shoulders. The Egyptians washed frequently and put on clean clothes often, not just for special occasions. The plagues of frogs, lice, and flies sent by God were a terrible trial for the Egyptians.

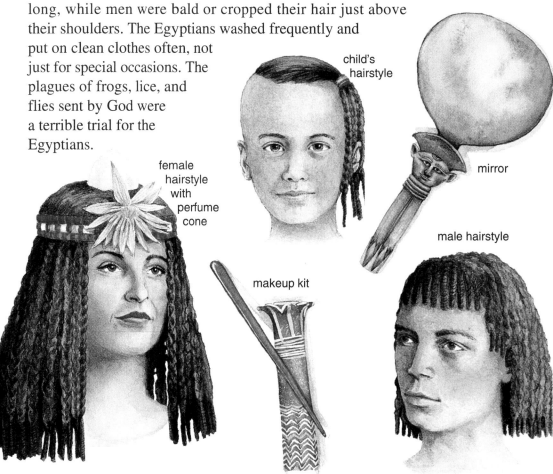

razor

child's hairstyle

mirror

female hairstyle with perfume cone

male hairstyle

makeup kit

Rami lay on the soft ground. The harvest was over, and now he could rest. All that mattered to him was that there was no more work until after the next flood of the Nile. It was good to be a farmer in Egypt.

The harvest celebration would be tomorrow night. Everyone would eat, sing, and play games. Rami knew many songs, and he had his own flute to play when others sang. His sister played a small harp that she held in her lap. One of the older boys had a *sistrum,* an instrument made of metal rods attached to a metal frame. It was like a huge rattle.

Rami's mother had made new clothing and purchased cosmetics for the whole family. Rami knew his sister had a new wig to wear. His mother would wear a small cone of perfumed oil on her head. During the evening the melting cone would cover her head and shoulders in fragrant oil.

Rami glanced down at his dirty clothes. Mother will never let me in the house looking like this, he thought. He knew his mother would leave fresh clothes for him near the water bucket.

Rami thought of the little three-room house made of mud brick where he lived. The animals stayed in the first room, and the family lived in the other two. Maybe if it were cool this evening, he and his family would go up to the flat roof to enjoy the breezes.

Rami stood up and stretched his weary body. He walked toward home through the shorn fields, the Nile waters gleaming behind him in the last rays of sun.

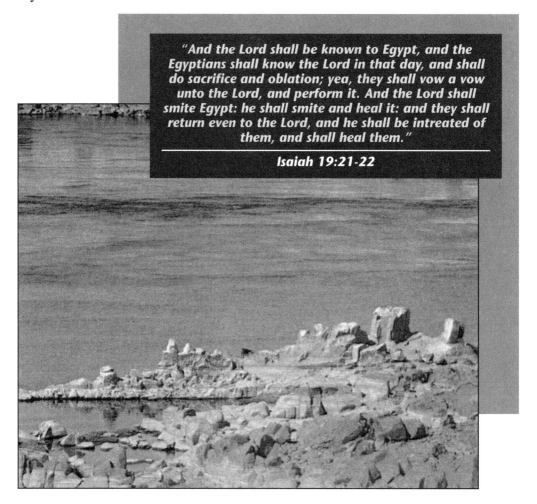

"And the Lord shall be known to Egypt, and the Egyptians shall know the Lord in that day, and shall do sacrifice and oblation; yea, they shall vow a vow unto the Lord, and perform it. And the Lord shall smite Egypt: he shall smite and heal it: and they shall return even to the Lord, and he shall be intreated of them, and shall heal them."

Isaiah 19:21-22

3

The People of One God:
Ancient Israel

A New Nation

The history of Israel begins with God's *covenant,* or special agreement, with Abraham. In about 2100 B.C., God called Abraham to leave his country. God promised to make Abraham's descendants into a great nation.

God led Abraham to the land of *Canaan.* Although there were a few cities in Canaan, many Canaanites were *nomads.* They wandered about the land, grazing their animals. Nomads lived in tents that could be moved easily from place to place. Do you think your family would like to live in a tent? Abraham and his family lived as nomads in Canaan.

God blessed Abraham with many servants and large flocks of sheep and herds of cattle. When Abraham was one hundred years old, God gave him a son, Isaac.

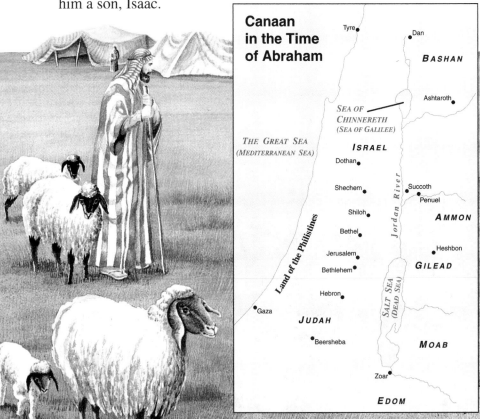

Canaan in the Time of Abraham

Tyre

Dan

BASHAN

Ashtaroth

SEA OF CHINNERETH
(SEA OF GALILEE)

THE GREAT SEA
(MEDITERRANEAN SEA)

ISRAEL

Dothan

Shechem

Succoth
Penuel

Jordan River

Shiloh

Bethel

AMMON

Jerusalem

Heshbon

Bethlehem

GILEAD

Hebron

SALT SEA
(DEAD SEA)

Gaza

JUDAH

Beersheba

MOAB

Land of the Philistines

Zoar

EDOM

Israel

Location—In the Middle East, on the eastern shore of the Mediterranean Sea. The ancient territory of Canaan is now held by four nations: Israel, Lebanon, Jordan, and Syria.

Climate—Temperate; mild winters and warm summers. Temperatures range from 48°F in the winter to 90°F in the summer. In the northern mountains, annual precipitation may reach 40 inches, while in the southern deserts little or no rain falls.

Topography—Five major land regions run north to south. The lowland coastal plain lies along the Mediterranean Sea. Rolling hills and valleys lead to the Lebanon Mountains in the northeast. The valley of the Jordan River lies to the east of these hills, and further east yet is a large plateau. A desert, the final region, is found in the southeast.

Natural Resources—Modern Israel has few natural resources. Some petroleum and natural gas are available, and salt is mined near the Dead Sea. In ancient times, forests of cedar and other hardwoods were abundant.

Geography and Culture—Part of an area known as the Fertile Crescent, a crescent-shaped region surrounding the Tigris, Euphrates, and Jordan Rivers, provides rich soil for farming. There are few other sources of water; famine often followed times when rain was scarce. Because Canaan lay between Assyria and Egypt, it became both a trading route and a target for expansion for both of these ancient empires.

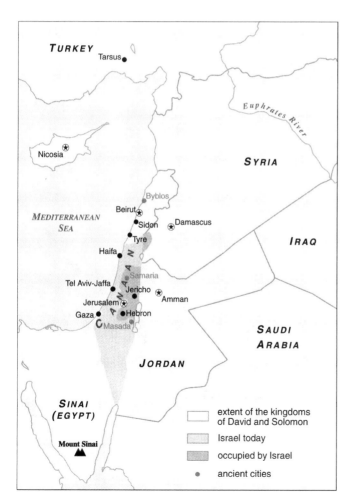

extent of the kingdoms of David and Solomon

Israel today

occupied by Israel

• ancient cities

51

God blessed Isaac and his son Jacob as He had blessed Abraham. Do you know how this group came to be known as the children of Israel? When Jacob surrendered to God's will, God gave him a new name: Israel.

One of Jacob's twelve sons was Joseph. Joseph became a slave in Egypt when his brothers sold him to passing merchants. God blessed Joseph by causing the pharaoh to put him in charge of Egypt's grain store- houses. In this position, Joseph was second to the pharaoh in the land of Egypt. When famine drove the rest of Joseph's family from Canaan, Joseph gave them food and a home in Egypt. They would not return to Canaan for four hundred years.

Eventually, a pharaoh who had not known Joseph became ruler of Egypt. He grew angry with the Israelites, or *Hebrews,* because they were more in number and mightier than the Egyptians. He made them his slaves.

Then the pharaoh decreed that all Hebrew boy babies must be killed. One boy was saved when his mother put him into a basket on the Nile River. The pharaoh's daughter took him from the river and named him *Moses,* which means "drawn from the water."

When Moses was eighty years old, God told him that he would be the one to lead the Israelites back into the land He had promised to Abraham, Isaac, and Jacob.

Do you think the pharaoh was willing to let the people of Israel go? No, he said that he did not know Moses' God, and he would not obey Him. God sent terrible diseases and destruction upon Egypt. The story of these *plagues* can be read in the Bible, beginning in Exodus 7:20.

The tenth plague—death of the first-born of every family—was the most terrible. Moses instructed the Hebrews to spread the blood of a lamb on the doorposts of each house. In every house not covered by blood, the first-born child died. Pharaoh's first-born son died in the plague. At last, pharaoh agreed to let the Hebrews go.

Jews celebrate Passover each year to commemorate the deliverance from slavery in Egypt.

God led the Israelites across the desert toward the land of Canaan. At Mount Sinai, God gave Moses the *law.* He told the Israelites to build a place for worship called the *tabernacle.* The tabernacle was a symbol of God's presence with His people.

Daily the priests sacrificed animals on the altar of the tabernacle. And once each year, the high priest entered the most holy place to sprinkle blood on the mercy seat. Why was the blood sacrifice necessary? It was a picture of Christ's blood that would be shed on the cross.

> *"And every priest standeth daily ministering and offering oftentimes the same sacrifices, which can never take away sins: but this man, after he had offered one sacrifice for sins for ever, sat down on the right hand of God."*
>
> **Hebrews 10:11-12**

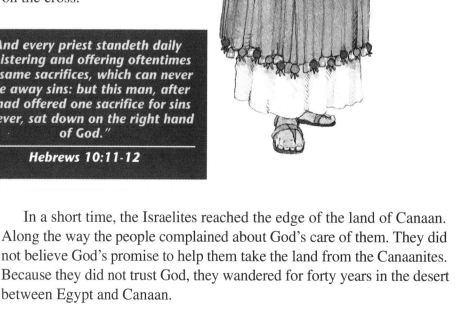

In a short time, the Israelites reached the edge of the land of Canaan. Along the way the people complained about God's care of them. They did not believe God's promise to help them take the land from the Canaanites. Because they did not trust God, they wandered for forty years in the desert between Egypt and Canaan.

◆ DISCOVERING HOW ◆

To Work with a Research Team

1. You and your research team will need a Bible, a pencil, a ruler, and a sheet of drawing paper.

2. Read the passage your teacher assigns you about one of the furnishings of the tabernacle. Take notes as you read, writing down details of the item's appearance, as well as its dimensions and location in the tabernacle if given.

3. With your research team, compare notes and make a drawing of the piece of furniture, keeping it as close as possible to the biblical description.

4. Choose one member of your research team to show your team's drawing to the rest of the class and to give any details you found.

The Law of God

The thing that set the Israelites apart from all other people was their belief in the true God, *Yahweh* or Jehovah. God ruled His people directly. Direct rule by God is called a *theocracy,* from the Greek words *theos* meaning "god" and *kratos* meaning "power."

In most ancient cultures, the laws were made by the king or ruler. In Israel, the laws were made by God. The best known part of the law is the Ten Commandments, found in Exodus 20. How many do you know?

Modern tourists visit the traditional site of Mt. Sinai, the place where God gave the law to Moses.

Today, the laws of many Western countries are "echoes" of the law given to Moses. Why do you think the laws of the Israelites have had such an effect on the laws of other lands? Unlike laws written by man, God's laws are perfect.

Inhabiting the Promised Land

After Moses died in about 1400 B.C., Joshua led the Israelites into the land of Canaan. God commanded the Israelites to destroy all the Canaanites. Joshua assigned each of the twelve tribes of Israel a portion of the land. Each tribe was supposed to destroy the Canaanites in its part of the land. Many Canaanites were destroyed or driven away, but some were left alone. Do you think God was pleased?

The Hebrews began to worship Canaanite gods. God punished the Israelites for this idolatry by making them subjects of the people they had not destroyed. In defeat, God's people called to Him for deliverance. God sent deliverers, called *judges*. Even when the judges brought peace to the land, the people did not remain faithful to God.

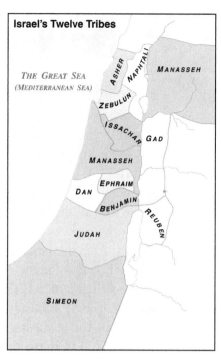

Israel's Twelve Tribes

THE GREAT SEA (MEDITERRANEAN SEA)

ASHER
NAPHTALI
MANASSEH
ZEBULUN
ISSACHAR
GAD
MANASSEH
EPHRAIM
DAN
BENJAMIN
REUBEN
JUDAH
SIMEON

The pattern of disobedience and punishment followed by repentance and deliverance continued for more than three hundred years. Finally, the people of Israel began to believe that the problems with their enemies could be solved only one way. They asked the last judge, Samuel, to give them a king like the other nations.

Samson, one of the judges of Israel, personally killed many of the Philistines during his lifetime.

57

Smelting Iron

Swords, javelins, arrowheads, and spearheads hung on the smithy's blackened walls. Nails, knives, sickles, and axes decorated the crude shelves in the small Israeli shop. But it had not always been so.

Before 1100 B.C., the Philistines controlled the iron industry. Anyone in Canaan who wanted an iron weapon or tool had to purchase it from a Philistine ironsmith. The Philistines kept the secret of smelting iron from those around them.

In later years the Israelites made their own weapons by smelting the iron. They had to mine *ore*—a rock or mineral that contains something valuable, such as a metal. Then they smelted the iron by heating the ore and adding different substances to separate the iron from the ore. After purifying the iron with intense heat, the ironsmiths poured the liquefied metal into a clay or stone mold. On other occasions they would hammer it into the desired shape.

> *"Behold, I have created the smith that bloweth the coals in the fire, and that bringeth forth an instrument for his work; . . . No weapon that is formed against thee shall prosper; . . . This is the heritage of the servants of the Lord."*
>
> **Isaiah 54:16-17**

No longer did the Philistines limit Israel's use of weapons or tools. The Israelites could now mine the ore and smelt the iron themselves. But even with this advantage over their enemies, ultimately God was their protector.

Life in the Promised Land

God commanded the Israelite parents to teach their children. What things do your parents teach you? The most important thing Israelite parents taught their children was the law of God.

Parents also taught their children practical skills. Fathers taught their sons a trade and how to work the farm and tend the animals. Mothers taught their daughters to cook, make clothing, tend a garden, and make goods to sell.

> "And these words, which I command thee this day, shall be in thine heart: and thou shalt teach them diligently unto thy children, and shalt talk of them when thou sittest in thine house, and when thou walkest by the way, and when thou liest down, and when thou risest up."
>
> **Deuteronomy 6:6-7**

Gerrit van Honthorst, Holy Family in the Carpenter Shop, *The Bob Jones University Collection*

God warned the Israelites that a king would take their sons for his armies. He would take their daughters to work in his palace. He would take their land and their crops to feed his servants and armies. Still, the people wanted a king.

God chose Saul to be Israel's first king about 1020 B.C. At first it seemed that Saul would defeat the *Philistines,* Israel's worst enemies. Then Saul disobeyed the instructions of the Lord. Although Saul was king for many more years, he never led the Israelites to victory as the people had hoped.

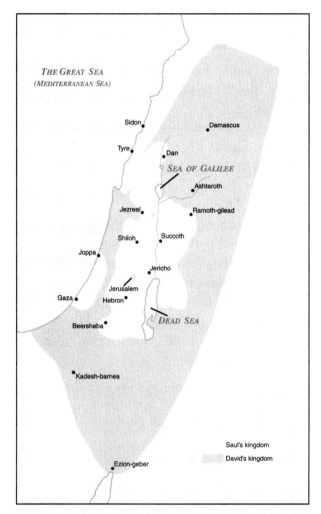

THE GREAT SEA
(MEDITERRANEAN SEA)

Sidon

Damascus

Tyre

Dan

SEA OF GALILEE

Ashtaroth

Jezreel

Ramoth-gilead

Shiloh

Succoth

Joppa

Jericho

Jerusalem

Gaza

Hebron

DEAD SEA

Beersheba

Kadesh-barnea

Saul's kingdom

David's kingdom

Ezion-geber

God appointed a new king—David—in the place of Saul. Under King David, the Philistine armies were finally defeated. David also captured the Canaanite city of Jerusalem. At David's death in 961 B.C., his son Solomon became king. Solomon made *treaties,* or peace agreements, with many other countries. During Solomon's reign, the people of Israel had peace.

Solomon built storehouses, palaces, and forts throughout Israel. His most impressive project was the temple in Jerusalem. It was built from huge stones and cedar timbers from the Lebanon Mountains. Decorations were made from ivory, gold, and precious stones.

Solomon made peace treaties with other countries by marrying the daughters of foreign kings. Solomon had seven hundred wives, including Ammonite, Phoenician, and Egyptian princesses. Each wife brought with her a false god.

The Phoenicians

One Canaanite group was the *Phoenicians.* Tyre, Sidon, and Byblos are Phoenician cities mentioned in the Bible. The Phoenicians were prosperous traders, craftsmen, and businessmen.

The hills of Phoenicia were covered with forests—the famous cedars of Lebanon. David used wood from these forests when he built his palace, and Solomon included Lebanon cedar in the construction of the temple in Jerusalem.

The wicked Queen Jezebel, daughter of a Phoenician king, brought idol worship to Israel after her marriage to Ahab. She supported 450 priests of Baal, the storm god. Many Israelites turned to the worship of Baal.

The prophet Ezekiel warned that the Phoenician city of Tyre would be destroyed and thrown into the sea. Can you guess what happened to Tyre? Nebuchadnezzar destroyed it in 571 B.C. Years later, the remains were thrown into the sea to build a *causeway,* or land bridge, to the new island city of Tyre. The old city of Tyre was never rebuilt and is even today "like the top of a rock" (Ezekiel 26:14).

Ruins of Tyre

The Kingdom Divided

God required one thing of Solomon: to serve and worship Him. But Solomon's wives had turned his heart away from the Lord. At Solomon's death in 922 B.C., the ten northern tribes followed Jeroboam, one of Solomon's officials. The two southern tribes, Judah and Benjamin, were ruled by Solomon's son Rehoboam.

> "And if thou wilt walk before me, as David thy father walked, in integrity of heart, and in uprightness, to do according to all that I have commanded thee, and wilt keep my statutes and my judgments: then I will establish the throne of thy kingdom upon Israel for ever, as I promised to David thy father, saying, There shall not fail thee a man upon the throne of Israel."
>
> **I Kings 9:4-5**

Divided Kingdom

Tyre
Dan
SYRIA (ARAM)
PHOENICIA
Kedesh
Hazor
SEA OF GALILEE
Bashan
THE GREAT SEA (MEDITERRANEAN SEA)
Megiddo
Jezreel
Dothan
Jabesh-gilead
Jordan River
ISRAEL
Samaria
Shechem
Succoth
Joppa
Shiloh
AMMON
Bethel
Gilgal
Jericho
Ashdod
Jerusalem
Heshbon
Ashkelon
Bethlehem
PHILISTIA
Hebron
DEAD SEA
Gaza
En-gedi
JUDAH
Beersheba
MOAB
EDOM

Northern Kingdom
Southern Kingdom

The northern tribes took the name *Israel.* Jeroboam established his capital at *Samaria.* To keep his people from returning to Jerusalem to worship, he made two golden calves and proclaimed them the gods of Israel. None of Israel's nineteen kings over the next two hundred years served the Lord. In 722 B.C. Israel was conquered by Assyria.

The Southern Kingdom took the name *Judah.* Judah's kings were all descendants of King David. Some of these kings were wicked, but a few of Judah's rulers did "that which was right in the sight of the Lord."

In 586 B.C., Nebuchadnezzar, king of Babylon, conquered Judah. He destroyed Jerusalem, including the temple. He took more than ten thousand people away to *exile* in Babylonia. Daniel and his friends Shadrach, Meshach, and Abednego were among the Babylonian exiles. Many of those who were left behind fled into Egypt, Moab, Samaria, and other countries. This scattering of the Judeans—or Jews as they became known—into many other nations is known as the dispersion, or *diaspora.*

God's People in Exile

In Babylon the Jews had no temple. Small groups met together in *synagogues,* where priests instructed them in the *Torah,* the first five books of the Bible.

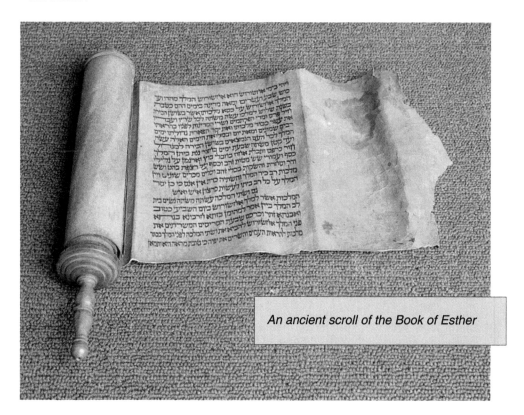

An ancient scroll of the Book of Esther

During the reign of King Ahasuerus, Haman, a greedy palace official, grew angry with a Jew named Mordecai. Haman decided to take revenge on Mordecai by plotting to kill all the Jews of Babylon. But Esther, a Jew, had become queen. Esther risked her life to plead with the king to save her people from destruction. King Ahasuerus gave the Jews the right to defend themselves from anyone who would try to hurt or kill them. He also ordered the execution of Haman.

"And in every province, and in every city, whithersoever the king's commandment and his decree came, the Jews had joy and gladness, a feast and a good day."

Esther 8:17

After Haman's death, the Jews held a great feast, sent each other presents, and gave gifts to poor people. Today this holiday is called *Purim* and is celebrated by Jews around the world.

Rebuilding the Nation

Cyrus the Great of Persia conquered Babylon in 539 B.C. He allowed the Jews to return to Judah. Do you think all the Jews returned to their homeland? Not all did. Many stayed in Babylon where they had made their homes.

The first group that returned to Judah was discouraged by what it found. The Jews who had remained in Judah during the exile were not willing to help rebuild Jerusalem. Not until 515 B.C. was the temple finally rebuilt.

Alexander the Great defeated the Persians in 331 B.C., and the land of Judea became part of Alexander's empire. Greek rulers brought new ideas and laws to the Jews. Many Jews felt that as long as they were allowed to worship God, the changes in culture would not matter.

Alexander the Great

In 176 B.C. Antiochus IV became ruler of Judea. He outlawed obedience to God's law. Keeping the Sabbath became punishable by death. It was against the law to own a copy of the Torah. Antiochus even set up idols in the temple and sacrificed pigs on the altar of God.

Altars to false gods were set up in many Jewish cities, including the small town of Modin. As the people of Modin watched to see what would happen, a Syrian official commanded a Jew to bow down to the altar. When he bowed, the priest Mattathias jumped out of the crowd and killed the man. He also killed the Syrian official and destroyed the altar. Mattathias knew his life was in danger. He and his five grown sons escaped to the mountains, where they gathered a group of three thousand fighting men.

Mattathias died in 166 B.C. His third son, Judah, took his place of leadership. Judah, called Judah Maccabeus ("the hammer"), led surprise attacks throughout the countryside. In one battle, he defeated the Syrians and burned their camp. Finally, in 164 B.C., the Syrians stopped persecuting the Jews. However, pagan gods were still worshiped in the temple.

In December 164 B.C. the Maccabees took Jerusalem. They destroyed the idols and all evidence of pagan worship. Exactly three years after the first pagan sacrifice was offered, the priests again offered an unblemished lamb to God. The rededication of the temple was celebrated for eight days. Judah Maccabeus declared that this festival, Hanukkah, should be celebrated every year with gladness and joy.

The Menorah is featured during the celebration of the Jewish holiday Hanukkah.

During this time, two groups of scholars became important in Judea, the Pharisees and the Sadducees. The Pharisees stressed complete obedience to the law. The Sadducees were more willing to accept the ideas and customs of the secular rulers of Israel—first the Greeks and then the Romans.

Which of these groups do you think was more popular with the common people in Israel? Many thought of the Pharisees as the perfect example of holiness. But Jesus condemned both groups. He knew their good works were nothing more than rituals, and their hearts were cold.

"Woe unto you, scribes and Pharisees, hypocrites! for ye are like unto whited sepulchers, which indeed appear beautiful outward, but are within full of dead men's bones, and of all uncleanness. Even so ye also outwardly appear righteous unto men, but within ye are full of hypocrisy and iniquity."

Matthew 23:27-28

By the time Jesus was born, the Greek Empire had been overthrown by the Roman Empire. Although some Jews in Judea had become used to the idea of foreign rule, many wanted independence. Some of these people spoke against the Roman government. Some—the Zealots—actually planned to rebel against the government.

Jesus Christ preached and performed miracles throughout Judea, proving that He was the Son of God. He kept the entire law of God and died a perfect death on the cross. In His death, He paid the penalty of the law for the sins of His people. Looking for salvation from the oppressive government, most of the Jews did not recognize Jesus as Messiah. They continued to hope for an earthly Messiah to free them from the Romans, not a heavenly Redeemer to save them from their sins.

"He came unto his own, and his own received him not."

John 1:11

Possible site of the Crucifixion

In A.D. 70, Emperor Vespasian looked out from his palace in Rome and considered his empire. He ruled lands as far away as Britain and India. Only the Jews refused to adopt Roman ways and worship Roman gods. Vespasian decided to destroy the Jews.

Led by Vespasian's son Titus, the Roman army surrounded Jerusalem and waited. At first the Jews within the city felt secure. They believed God would send them a deliverer, that perhaps now Messiah would come. Then famine set in. Many Jews ate grass and gnawed on leather shoes to keep from dying.

The Wailing Wall (left) is all that remains of the temple complex in Jerusalem.

At last the Romans broke down the wall and marched through Jerusalem, killing all the Jews they met and destroying building after building. Many Jews still hoped that Messiah would save them, but when they saw the temple in flames, they despaired. Old men wept as the building burned. Soldiers looted the temple, stealing the golden candlesticks, the table of showbread, and thousands of gold and silver coins from the temple treasury. Jerusalem was destroyed. The Romans had conquered all of Judea with one exception—Masada.

Masada still sits atop its hill in Israel.

Masada

Nearly one thousand Jews lived at Masada, a fort city overlooking the Dead Sea. They believed they were safe from the Romans because they had plenty of food and water, and the Roman army could not attack them. The only trail up to Masada was narrow and winding. If the Roman soldiers attempted to come up this trail, the Jews could kill them one by one. And, although they could see soldiers camped below them, the Jews knew that the summer heat would soon force the Romans to leave.

But the Romans did not give up. Using tons of earth, they built a huge ramp up to the walls of Masada. Then they used a battering ram to break down the outer wall. The soldiers then shot fiery arrows against the timbers of the inner wall. At first the wind caused the flames to blow back against the Roman invaders. Then, as evening set in, the wind shifted and the wall caught fire. The Jews despaired. Their cause was lost.

The Roman soldiers decided to attack in the morning. That night, the Jews of Masada met together around a fire. Their leader told them it would be better to die in freedom than to be killed by the Romans. The Jews agreed. The Jews chose ten men to carry out the executions. When only the ten men were left alive, they chose one man to kill the other nine. How do you think that man felt as he looked on his family and friends lying dead around him? Do you think he changed his mind about dying? He did not.

The next morning the Romans burst in upon Masada, expecting a fight. They were met by silence. Then two women crept out of a cellar. They told the Romans what had happened and led them to the bodies. The Romans stood in silence at the sight of 960 Jews who died on the last day of Masada's defense.

The Jews' resistance ended with the defeat of Masada. But the life of Israel, in the study of the Torah and the ancient worship of God, went on as Jews settled all over the world. They also took with them the hope of a coming Messiah. So long the servants of other nations, the Jews anxiously awaited His coming. Unfortunately, most Jews had formed their own ideas of what Messiah should be like, and they did not recognize Him when He came.

Today, not one of ancient Israel's beautiful buildings remains. The gifts of Israel to the world are far greater than mere arts and crafts, monuments, language, or ideas. Israel's gifts are God's gifts: His Word, the Bible, and the Word, God's precious Son.

Scenes of Israel, including a source of the Jordan River (left)

Mysteries of the Indus:
Ancient India

The sun is starting to rise over a distant hill. It is a sandy hill that stands behind the scene below. Dark-skinned men in flowing robes murmur in the hush of the early morning as they swing shovels rhythmically into the earth. Suddenly—like a rush of wind—the murmur rises to an excited buzz. They have found something!

The supervisor walks slowly to the spot where the helpers have dug. Each step is calm and deliberate. He cannot get too excited—it could be a false alarm. He kneels beside the hard brick that one of the nationals has uncovered. The supervisor removes a small, delicate brush from the satchel that is slung over his shoulder. He gently sweeps the brick. Terra cotta! He leans closer, using his magnifying glass to examine the terra cotta piece.

Slowly, so slowly, the supervisor's eyes swing upward. He stares at the distant hill, the air blurring with the sun's now bright heat. "It is Mohenjo-Daro," he whispers to the distant hill. "We have found the Indus."

One of the greatest archaeological finds occurred in India during the 1920s. This find was the discovery of *Mohenjo-Daro* and its sister city, *Harappa.* These cities have been dated to approximately 2500 B.C. Do you know how long ago that was?

Archaeological digs do not always uncover secrets from the past. Archaeologists may spend years studying and searching for ancient civilizations. They may excavate site after site, only to end up empty-handed. Mohenjo-Daro and Harappa were different, however. The discovery of these two ancient cities opened the door to a world long forgotten—the world of the Indus Valley civilization. Why do you think this discovery was so important to archaeologists and historians? The discovery of artifacts belonging to these ancient peoples began the unraveling of the mystery that envelopes our past.

Ruins of Mohenjo-Daro

The year is 1925. A young man sits at a makeshift desk made of empty crates. The flap of his tent stirs with a sudden breeze. His pen scratches the paper at a furious pace. Occasionally, he stops and stares thoughtfully at a small photograph propped against a dusty hat.

"My dear Lucy," he writes, smiling at the name that brings so many memories to mind. "I do miss you and Mother and the children. Though I yearn to be with you all, my trip here to India is necessary for my ancient history studies. The exciting discoveries by Sir John Marshall here make this site one of the most desirable places for study. He is a very knowledge-able man to work for. Five officers work under him, including my supervisor, Mr. Hargreaves."

"You asked me about some of the strange sights I have seen. No, I haven't seen any cobras or men on beds of nails since we left the big city of Karachi where we first docked. Here in Mohenjo-Daro we are far away from any big cities. But I rather like this peaceful area with its rolling hills. The hills remind me of southern England. Yet everything here is dry and yellow with dust—how I miss green England!"

William pauses and gazes between the tent flaps at the late afternoon sky. "The weather here has been perfect for the dig," he writes. "Now is the dry, cool season in India. Our temperatures are in the fifties, which is perfect for outdoor work. The Indians tell me that during the hot season, temperatures rise to over 100°. Quite warm, wouldn't you say? At any rate, Mohenjo-Daro is a splendid place to excavate. I must leave off for now to prepare for tomorrow's work. Do write again. Give my love to Mother and the others."

India

Location—A large peninsula in south-central Asia, jutting out into the Indian Ocean above the equator. Modern India is bordered by Pakistan in the northwest. China, Nepal, Bhutan, Burma, and Bangladesh are on the eastern and north-eastern borders.

Climate—Primarily temperate, with patches of tropical and dry climates. Affected by yearly *monsoons,* or winds that bring wet air in the summer and dry air in the winter. Temperatures are above 70°F most of the year, except in the north. Annual precipitation ranges from zero to over four hundred inches.

Topography—Contains three major land regions. The Himalaya Mountains stretch across northeastern India, cutting off India and some of her neighbors from the rest of the continent. In so doing, they create what is called the Indian subcontinent. South of the mountains is the northern plain, watered by three rivers: the Indus, the Ganges, and the Brahmaputra. Southern India is a large plateau called Deccan.

Natural Resources—Large deposits of iron ore and some coal. Small amounts of other minerals, including uranium, diamonds, emeralds, gold, and silver. There is also much fertile land.

Geography and Culture—The Indus and Ganges riverbanks provided the first homes for the ancient civilizations of India. The rivers supplied water, fish, and transportation. The mountains of northern India have also influenced India's history. Only through the passes in the northwest could foreigners invade India, which they have done regularly throughout history. Because desert and rough terrain lie south of the river valleys, invaders rarely penetrated farther south. Most of India's history has taken place in northern India.

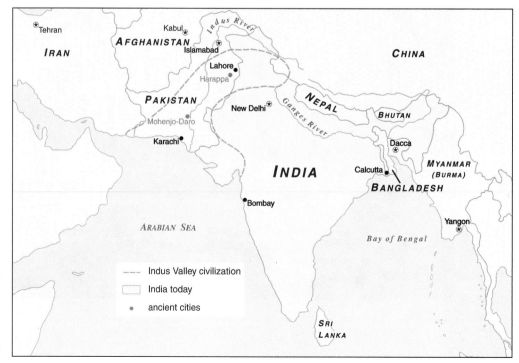

William wrote his letters in 1925, but his work took him back through time, placing him in a civilization that existed thousands of years ago. Locate Mohenjo-Daro on the map on page 78. Can you guess the name of the ancient civilization that lived there? It is sometimes called the *Harappan* civilization after the Pakistani town of Harappa—the site where archaeological evidence was first found.

Historians believe that the people of Harappa were very similar to those who lived nearly four hundred miles away at Mohenjo-Daro. Similar artifacts were found in both locations, indicating that both cities were part of the same civilization. Why do you think this is true? For about eight hundred years these ancient Indians flourished in the fertile river valley.

The Indus River

At first, historians and archaeologists could only speculate about this ancient civilization. Later, artifacts found in the 1920s indicated that the Indus people were highly sophisticated. Because of its closeness to the river, the land was good for farming and raising animals. Around 2500 B.C. some of the first communities were formed in the Indus Valley. Archaeologists have found in these villages well-organized, two-story houses that included a bathing area and a drainage system that ran throughout the entire city. How is this design similar to your town or city?

More artifacts, such as gold ornaments, bronze utensils, and bronze pots, led archaeologists to believe that the Indus people were artistic and skilled craftsmen. Many of these ornaments contain pictographs, but these ancient writings remain an unsolved mystery even today.

In this view of Mohenjo-Daro, the large area at the center left is called the Great Bath.

William watches the helpers record and label each artifact that has been found. It is getting to be late afternoon. He wipes his damp forehead, leaving a smudge of yellow dust. He sits down at the corner table to jot a few lines to his sister. "Dear Lucy," he writes. "I'm glad to hear your schoolwork is going better. Keep studying hard. I'm also pleased that you are reading about India. We have many native boys and girls about your age working for us. They carry away baskets of soil from the dig. The carriers often search the dirt in their baskets in hopes of finding more artifacts for which they will receive an extra reward above their usual wage."

William smiles. "I bet you would enjoy that job as well! I am taking a short break now, but our work here at Mohenjo-Daro continues. Mr. Hargreaves assigned me to help excavate a particular house. We believe there is an entire city buried in this area, but my house is House VIII on what we call High Lane. It seems that Mohenjo-Daro had two main streets. Much of the remains we have found appear to have been middle-class houses owned by merchants and craftsmen. It must have been a prosperous city."

William pauses, watching the helpers tag a bronze pot. "When I come home," he writes, continuing his letter, "I'll bring sketches of House VIII. The first floor is made of red brick. We believe at one time it had a second story of wood. We think that because of the charred bits of wood we have found along the top of the brick. The house has an open courtyard to let in light.

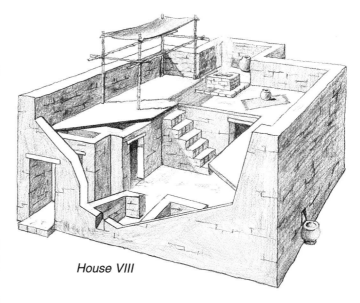

House VIII

There are small rooms off the courtyard, one for the well and the other for a bathroom. The Indus people had advanced plumbing! Other rooms were probably used as kitchens and guest rooms. The family's sleeping quarters were in the back and upstairs."

William pauses. The helpers have moved on to tagging shell-like utensils. "House VIII contained some interesting artifacts," he continues. "Some of our finds from it include a spoon made from a shell, a small clay ball, a pretty ring, and some grain kernels. We also found several pieces of sculpted alabaster. Putting them together, we discovered they formed the figure of a man. We don't know whether it was used as an idol for worship or as a piece of art. Right now, it is one of the earliest Indian sculptures we have."

"Each artifact must first be photographed where it was found, then labeled, and then removed. Then we record all our artifacts to keep track of them."

The helpers stir, putting the artifacts carefully away. William glances at his watch. "I must leave off for now, Lucy. I had meant for this to be only a brief letter. As you can see, we are very busy, but it is so exciting to uncover pieces of the past. It is like catching glimpses of a secret and silent world. Keep up with your studies like a good girl! I shall write again soon."

To Catalog an Artifact

1. Get Notebook page 24 and the following supplies: a resealable plastic bag, a self-adhesive label, a pencil, a permanent marking pen, a postal scale, a meter stick, and a metric ruler.

2. Carefully examine the "artifact" your teacher has given you.

3. Complete the catalog sheet based on your study of the artifact.

4. Follow your teacher's instructions for safe storage of the artifact.

Some time has passed since William's last letter. The dig uncovers more and more artifacts that tell about the ancient Indus. "Dear Lucy," writes William. "It has been some time since I last wrote. Our finds are increasing almost every day, it seems. Since my last letter, we have found more artifacts. We have pieces of jewelry made from gold and precious stones. We also have children's toys, several standard weights made of stone, and of course, many pottery fragments."

Drawings of Indus seals

"Several interesting items in the collection are small seals carved with pictures and the Indus script. They are made from *terra cotta,* a type of clay, or from *steatite,* a type of soapstone. The seals were probably used to identify an owner's goods. Unfortunately, we have been unable to decipher the script. A man here who specializes in *linguistics,* the study of languages, thinks it may be a long time before the Indus pictographs can be translated. We would know much more about these people if we could read their writing. One thing we would know is the purpose of a large building excavated by Sir John. We call it the Great Bath because it is a hall with a large sunken pool. We think it may have been used for religious purposes or for bathing. Until we can read the Indus script, we will not know for certain."

William's lamp flickers, causing shadows to shiver on the side of his tent. "One of our most interesting discoveries was a group of skeletons that we found in one room. There were fourteen in all. Although this may have been a burial room, it is more likely the scene of a tragedy—perhaps an indication that they were invaded by another people. Finding those bones  reminded me that there was more to the ancient Indus civilization than just interesting artifacts. Real people walked these streets and cooked in these pots."

William pauses, thoughtfully rubbing his chin. "I often wonder what they were really like—these dwellers of Mohenjo-Daro. Sometimes I walk on the ancient streets—just dirt paths now—and wonder whether there was a young man my age who walked this same way long ago. And if there was, what made him and his people vanish so quickly as the evidence seems to indicate?" William shakes himself a little as his lamp grows dimmer.

He glances at his lamp and writes quickly. "But, Lucy, this must remain one of those unsolved mysteries of the past. We must content ourselves with what we do know. I must go now and fetch more oil for my lamp—it shall soon be out. I will write again if we uncover any more interesting things. Take care."

The mystery that surrounds the ancient Indus people deepened as archaeologists uncovered more and more artifacts. It seems that this civilization came to a sudden halt between 1700 and 1500 B.C. Archaeologists believe that the Indus people suddenly disappeared from India. There could be a variety of reasons for the disappearance of these sophisticated, well-organized people. Flood, famine, or invasion by other peoples could have driven the inhabitants of Mohenjo-Daro from their homes.

One major cause for the disappearance of the Indians may have been an invasion by another people from the north. These people were *nomads,* or wanderers, and called themselves *Arya,* which means "noble."

The Aryans were warlike people who came into India with horses, chariots, and weapons. They spread across northern India and settled down into villages. Their way of life became the characteristic culture of ancient—and modern—India.

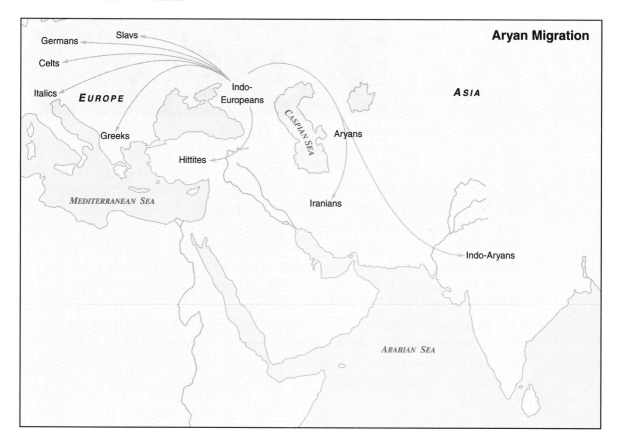

Aryan Migration

Village Life

The Aryans in India did not form a strong central government. Rather, India was made up of many independent villages first settled by the Aryans. Each settlement had a village council of the leading men of the village. The most important man in the village held the office of headman. The council and headman governed the village.

Every village had farmers and craftsmen. The craftsmen made necessary tools and household items for the villagers. They also produced artwork, much of which reflected religion. Sculptures of gods and goddesses were very common and were probably used in worship.

Modern Indian farmers grow much of the world's rice.

Most ancient Indians farmed for a living. Their success depended upon the yearly rains of the wet season—June to September. In India the rains come with the *monsoons,* yearly winds that blow from the west and bring moisture off the ocean. Once over land, the water vapor in the air condenses and falls as rain. If the rains are late or small, drought and famine may occur.

Aryans Throughout History

Throughout history, the term *Aryan* has assumed different meanings. The original Aryans were those light-skinned people who invaded India from the north. We can trace the echoes of these ancient peoples' name even in modern times. Thousands of years later—in the twentieth century—the term *Aryan* came to describe the people of Hitler's Germany.

Adolf Hitler borrowed from a French philosopher the idea that there is a master race. He believed that the northern European people were the most important race. Hitler called them Aryans. He believed that other races—particularly the Jews—did not deserve to live, so he started executing them. Today, the term *Aryan* is associated with Hitler and the racist ideas he represented. Do you remember what major war Hitler was involved in?

The Aryan name was not all that Hitler borrowed from the ancient Indians. He also borrowed one of their symbols. This symbol, the swastika, has been found on buildings and artifacts from ancient India as well as in places such as Turkey and Egypt. The term *swastika* in the Indian language, Sanskrit, means "a sign of good luck."

The swastika prominently displayed at one of Hitler's Nazi rallies

Religions of Ancient India

Hinduism

The Aryans, because they were nomads, probably encountered many different people and cultures in their travels. How do you think this interaction with other people affected the Aryans? As they settled in India, they adopted many beliefs and customs. The Aryans

Vishnu

developed a religion that would soon spread across India and that still exists today. Although this religion, *Hinduism,* was not formulated fully until after the time of Christ, its beliefs and practices quickly grew to influence the Indians' entire way of life.

Like many other ancient religions, Hinduism is *polytheistic,* or having many gods. The Hindus worship thousands of gods although they consider three gods to be the most important.

These three gods are *Brahma,* the Creator; *Shiva,* the Destroyer; and *Vishnu,* the Preserver.

Hindus believe that these three gods, in addition to thousands of others, are only different forms of the *World Soul,* a great spirit to which everything in the world—plants, animals, and gods—belongs. This belief is a form of *pantheism,* or the idea that there is deity in nature. How does this view of nature differ from the biblical description of God and creation?

Lakshmi, goddess of beauty, wealth, and good fortune

Hindus follow their religious practices diligently. They worship at Hindu temples and shrines, bring sacrifices and money to the priests, pray, and perform rituals. Some Hindus discipline their bodies to try to become holier. They seclude, starve, and inflict pain on themselves in an attempt to make their souls purer for the World Soul.

By following these practices, the Hindu hopes to be good enough to obtain salvation. Because these practices are part of a long process, another part of Hinduism is *reincarnation*. The Hindus believe that a reincarnated person lives more than once in different bodies—even in animals. Because of their belief in reincarnation, many Hindus will not eat certain animals, such as cattle. In some instances, they would rather starve than eat this type of meat.

A Hindu temple

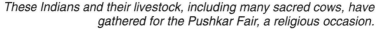

These Indians and their livestock, including many sacred cows, have gathered for the Pushkar Fair, a religious occasion.

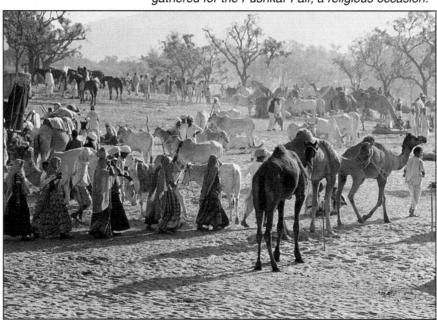

Families and Castes

Hinduism concerns itself not only with man's relationship to the gods but also with his relationship to other people. Because it teaches that everything is a part of the World Soul, Hinduism emphasizes the group above the individual. Social relationships in Hinduism center on the group. The two basic groups in India since the rise of Hinduism have been the family and the *caste,* or social class.

The core of Indian life was the family. When the Aryans settled in India, they encouraged large families. Families included more than just parents and their children. Grandparents, parents, sons, daughters-in-law, unmarried daughters, and grandchildren lived together in family *compounds* made up of several huts or houses.

The ancient Indians generally married when they were adults, not children. The oldest man in the family had complete authority over the other members. Everyone had to follow his orders. Hinduism teaches that complete obedience in the family is an important part of earning salvation.

Scenes from a Hindu wedding

91

The second important social group that every Indian belonged to was the *caste*. Castes were the classes of Indian society. Hindus believed that the higher a person was in the caste system, the closer he was to reuniting with the World Soul. Every Hindu hoped that his next rebirth would put him into a higher caste.

Hindu priests

There were four main caste divisions in Indian society. The highest was the priestly caste. When a member of this caste died, he supposedly reunited immediately with the World Soul. In this life, the priests held much power over the people because they directed most religious worship.

The caste of warriors and rulers came after the priestly caste. Farmers, traders, and laborers made up the third caste. Servants belonged to the lowest caste. Some Indians were outside the caste system. They were called *untouchables,* or *outcastes.* How do we use the word *outcast* today? Untouchables included any non-Hindu, anyone who worked with meat, and anyone who was expelled from his own caste. Within these four main castes there were hundreds of subcastes.

The caste had rules governing its members. The caste rules dictated whom one married, what clothing one wore, with whom one could eat, and what one's occupation was. In order to be reborn into a higher caste, a Hindu had to accept his present caste and the caste rules. A Hindu who did more or less than his caste demanded was unlikely to be reborn on a higher level. The caste system made Indian society very rigid. Today the caste system still exists in India, although it is not as rigid as it once was.

The Written Legacy

How do we know so much about early Hinduism? The early Indians left a written legacy called the *Vedas.* The Indian word *Veda* means "knowledge." The Vedas are the sacred books of Hinduism. The oldest Veda, the *Rig-Veda,* is believed to be one of the earliest known books, dating around the sixteenth century B.C.

The Rig-Veda, though difficult for modern man to understand, is a collection of the knowledge of the day. It includes hymns, prayers, poems, rituals, and philosophy. The existence of the Vedas, particularly the Rig-Veda, helps us to know that the people of the ancient Indus were sophisticated and enjoyed beauty and artistry.

In this Indian illustration, Brahma is shown at center left holding the Vedas.

Siddhartha Gautama

Not all Indians agreed with Hindu teachings, however. Near the end of the sixth century B.C., a man began to question Hindu beliefs. He disliked the caste system and the priests who ruled the people. He could not accept the Hindu belief that only members of the priestly caste were ready to reunite with the World Soul. This man, *Siddhartha Gautama,* decided that he was going to change Hinduism.

Gautama was born into a ruling family as a member of the warrior caste. Although he had many of the luxuries this world could offer, he was not satisfied. The poverty and pain he saw in the world bothered him. At the age of twenty-nine, he left his home to find a remedy for his own unhappiness and that of the world.

An Indian carving of the sleeping Buddha

For six years he lived in seclusion and near starvation but found no satisfactory answers. Then, according to the story, one day while meditating, Gautama became *enlightened* about the meaning of life. He assumed the name, *Buddha,* meaning "Enlightened One." Buddha developed his view of life through introducing what he called the *Four Noble Truths.* In these writings he proposed the concept that suffering can be overcome if a person does good works and ignores his desires. Buddhism also includes steps called *The Eightfold Path,* a list of good works that will help a person to achieve happiness and peace. Buddhism remains an important religion in India even today.

William sits at his desk, scribbling away. "Dear Lucy," he writes, "My time here at Mohenjo-Daro is almost over. Though I long to be in England once more, a part of me wants to stay excavating out on the field. I know I shall miss this place." He pauses and looks at the soft walls of his tent.

"I have learned so much here—so much about the ancient people who lived along the Indus, but how I want to learn more! There are many things we do not know—not just about the people at Mohenjo-Daro, but about ancient peoples around the world. Maybe someday—when you are older—you and I can return to India to find more about these ancient people. We could at least try. I must go for now and catch one last glimpse of the Indus. I shall see you soon. Love, William."

William rises from his desk and stands at his tent door. The buildings at the dig site are silhouettes against the reds and oranges of the setting sun. He takes a deep breath, listening to murmurings of the men who are finishing up at the site—or are those sounds voices from long ago? William smiles at his fancy. He will remember Mohenjo-Daro. He will never forget the mysteries of the Indus.

Dynasties in Seclusion:
Ancient China

Look back through the mist of thousands of years—back to an ancient civilization concealed among several mountain ranges, a large desert, and jungles. It is the ancient Chinese civilization, hidden from the rest of the world by *natural barriers.*

Throughout history, these barriers, or landforms that isolate a country from outside influence, kept the Chinese from having contact with other countries. How do you think this isolation affected China's culture? The Chinese were in no way behind the times. In fact, they were an advanced people, more skilled than other peoples of their day.

The ancient Chinese were ruled by several *dynasties.* A dynasty is a line of kings or rulers who belong to the same family. China, under these dynasties and in seclusion, began to flourish as a sophisticated society.

China

Location—Asia, or the Far East. China faces the Pacific Ocean in the east and Russia and Mongolia in the north. Pakistan, India, Nepal, Bhutan, Burma, Laos, and Vietnam border China on the west and south. North Korea also shares an eastern border with China.

Natural Resources—Large amounts of coal and oil, but both are under-developed. Contains deposits of tungsten, bauxite, iron ore, tin, lead, and mercury. The land has been heavily farmed and many of the original forests destroyed.

Climate—Most of China has a temperate climate. The northern regions are snowy. Climate is affected by yearly *monsoons,* or winds that bring rain. Annual precipitation ranges from twenty to eighty inches. Temperatures vary widely from region to region.

Topography—Three main land regions. The eastern region is the lowlands where the Huang He and Yangtze Rivers flow to the sea. In central China the land becomes rolling hills. The western third of China is hilly and mountainous. Tibet, in southwest China, has some of the highest mountain peaks in the world.

Geography and Culture—Civilization began along the major rivers, the Huang He and the Yangtze. Natural borders isolate China, limiting its contact with other countries in ancient times. Because of this isolation, the Chinese thought of themselves as the Central Kingdom, the only civilized kingdom on earth. This attitude affected much of China's culture.

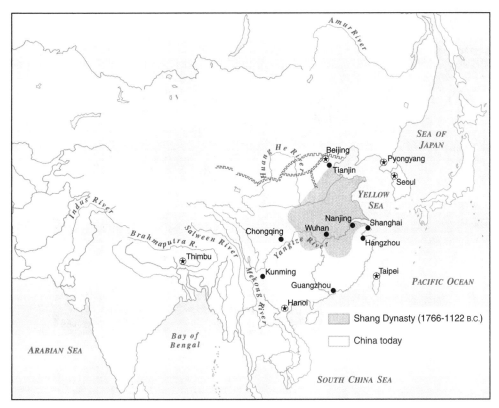

The Shang

One of the earliest dynasties in China was the Shang, ruling from 1766-1122 B.C. The Shang lived along the Huang He, or Yellow River, in northern China. Most of the common people in Shang China were farmers. The grains and vegetables they grew, especially rice, were necessary to feed the people. The Huang He was often called "China's Sorrow" because its many floods killed thousands of people and ruined many harvests.

The Shang people, particularly the royal family, practiced a religion that involved *ancestor worship.* The Shang believed that the spirits of their dead ancestors had power over them. When the weather was good, the Shang believed their ancestors were pleased. If *drought* or *famine* swept the land, the Shang thought they had angered their ancestors in some way. How do these beliefs differ from what the Bible teaches? The Bible teaches that there is only one God, and He has control over all things.

What do you think the Shang did to try to please their dead ancestors? They would make ornate bronze vessels called *tings* to cook meat as a sacrifice. Royal families had special ceremonies just to prepare and serve their sacrifices.

Ancestor worship shrines in modern China

The Bronze Age

Bronze Making

The tings were usually made from bronze as were ornaments and statues. Well over two thousand years before people in Europe made bronze, the Chinese developed special techniques in bronze smithing. Their skill as craftsmen has not been equalled, even today. Why do you think the Chinese did not share their knowledge of bronze making with other countries? For centuries, the natural barriers prevented trade and the spread of ideas.

Shang dynasty bronze ting (left) and another type of vessel, a kuang (above)

The Shang used a difficult process of bronze casting used by no other ancient people. First they made a mold of clay pieces that fit together into the shape of the piece to be cast. The detailed designs of the vessel were carved carefully into the clay. Some bronze smiths used ceramic molds.

After the molds were made, the bronze smith poured the molten bronze, consisting of copper, tin, and lead, into the molds. The smith had to work carefully to keep any air bubbles from entering the mixture. When the bronze hardened, the craftsman removed the mold pieces cautiously so that he could use them again. Once polished, the bronze vessel was ready to be used.

Besides using tings in ancestor worship, the Chinese also used *oracle bones*. An *oracle* was a message given by a person who the Chinese thought was a prophet or a god. Kings consulted priests and oracles before making decisions about planting, fighting, and building.

Oracle bones were pieces of bone or shell that priests heated with a hot metal rod. Cracks appeared, which supposedly revealed the ancestors' wishes. The priests then interpreted these cracks and reported the answers to the king. They also wrote the question and answer on the oracle bones and kept them for future reference.

The priests, who were also government officials, kept close watch on political and economic affairs. They made most of their interpretations in light of these current events. The priests had great power in the Shang dynasty because of the religious beliefs of the ancient Chinese. Oracle bones found by archaeologists today provide historical information about the Shang dynasty.

The Chou

The Shang dynasty ruled until 1122 B.C. At this time, a new family came into power—the Chou *(jō)*. The Chou dynasty ruled for about eight hundred years, lasting longer than any other dynasty in Chinese history.

Under the Chou, the Chinese developed an interest in education and literature. Chinese writing also developed in this period. Early writing in China consisted of *pictographs,* or pictures that are used in place of words. Pictographs were brushed on with fine strokes so that writing became a form of art.

The different pictographs used by the Chinese changed over time. Some pictographs combined to form a new word. A more common name for a pictograph is a *character.* What do we use to form words? We use letters. How many letters are in our alphabet? Our alphabet of twenty-six letters is simple compared to the Chinese system of writing. Chinese writing is not based on an alphabet but has about fifty thousand characters. Most Chinese today, however, know only about four thousand of these characters.

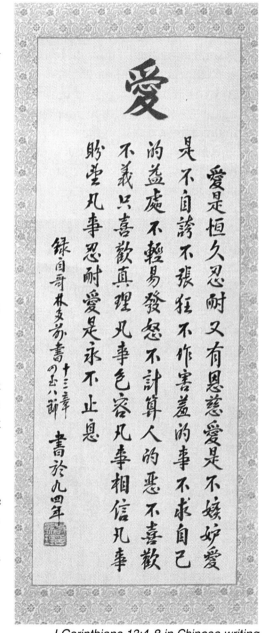

I Corinthians 13:4-8 in Chinese writing

103

The Classical Age

Another name for the rule of the Chou is the *Classical Age*. A *classic* is something that is thought to be the best of its kind and sets a standard of excellence. What do you think a Classical Age is, then? The Classical Age of China was a period that marked a high point in its cultural development. During this time, many important ideas and attitudes were formed that continue to affect the Chinese people today.

One man, Confucius, was a great influence in China during the Classical Age. He was a scholar and a teacher. His teachings were the most important ideas to come out of the Chinese Classical Age.

Confucius thought the key to having a peaceful society was to have every person know his place and act accordingly. He believed that society should be divided into classes, from peasants to nobility, and that this system would help people to get along better. Do you think that following Confucius's teachings completely can create a perfect society? Man, alone, cannot be perfect.

Confucius

"Not by works of righteousness which we have done, but according to his mercy he saved us, by the washing of regeneration, and renewing of the Holy Ghost."

Titus 3:5

Confucian beliefs may be considered a code of behavior. For example, Confucius taught about five important human relationships: (1) between king and subject, (2) between father and son, (3) between husband and wife, (4) between elder and younger brother, and (5) between friends.

In these relationships the younger and inferior person must always obey the elder and superior person. For example, a citizen must always obey the king, and a son must always obey his father. Can you think of verses in the Bible that teach similar values? Those who were the elder and superior, however, had to set a good example for those beneath them. The two main principles of Confucius's teaching, then, were being obedient and setting a good example.

Confucian teaching also emphasized the importance of the family. Several generations would live in one home. It was not uncommon for children to have grandparents or aunts and uncles living with them. Do you have any grandparents or aunts or uncles living in your home?

Classical Education

Confucius's teachings told people how to live a good life. After his death, his students collected their master's teachings and put them into a collection of sayings called the Confucian *Classics.*

One saying was "Learning without thought is a snare; thought without learning is a danger." What do you think this means? Confucius emphasized education as one way people could improve themselves and live better lives. During the Chou period, education became important. Chinese students spent many years learning the difficult Chinese language. Scholars held positions in government and were respected by the people.

Scholars during the Chou dynasty wrote many books. In addition to the Confucian *Classics,* these books are considered to be the classics of Chinese literature. Poetry, history, rituals, conduct, and music are some of the subjects found in books from this period. To be considered a true scholar in China, one had to have a thorough knowledge of these books. Many ancient Chinese books are based on Confucian teaching.

Classical Art

Artisans of the Chou dynasty continued to work with bronze. Chou bronze smiths, however, used a simpler method than the Shang used. The Chou produced fine works that still exist today. Much of their bronze work is covered with Chinese writing and intricate carvings of both real and imaginary animals.

The Chou, like the Shang, used their bronze works mainly in religious ceremonies, which often included placing the vessels in the tombs of ancestors. They also carved pieces of jade to create decorative pieces of art.

The Metropolitan Museum of Art, Rogers Fund, 1947 (47.27ab) Photograph©1979 The Metropolitan Museum of Art

Late Chou dynasty ritual vessels

Modern Chinese jade objects

As with other ancient peoples, music was important to the ancient Chinese. Music accompanied worship, work, and pleasure—even archery contests held by Chou nobles. One event used music to keep time for the shooting. If a contestant failed to shoot on the beat, the shot was disqualified.

The Ch'in

Government

After the Chou, the Ch'in dynasty was the next to rule, beginning about 221 B.C. Also spelled "Qin," the Ch'in dynasty was begun by the fierce emperor, Qin Shi Huangdi *(chǐn′ shē′ hwäng′dē′)*. Under his rule, China experienced many changes.

The Ch'in set up a *bureaucracy.* A bureaucracy is a system that gives a worker a job and then trains him for it, rather than passing on the job to a member of the family. In addition to this system, the Ch'in established one kind of money, standardized all measurements, and required all Chinese people to use the same writing. The emperor also took away land from the nobles, making it possible for both the poor and the rich to own land.

There were many changes in the Ch'in society at this time. How do you think these changes affected China? Although the changes helped to unify the country, Shi Huangdi used cruel and harsh methods to implement them. The Ch'in dynasty lasted less than thirty years. The reign of this powerful dynasty was short, yet it left a lasting monument, the name *China.* Can you see how China got its name?

Qin Shi Huangdi

The Great Wall

Perhaps the greatest accomplishment of the Ch'in period was the construction of the Great Wall. Shi Huangdi ordered the wall to be built by connecting a series of walls that were already standing. Stretching for more than fifteen hundred miles, the wall was designed to keep out invaders from the north, but it also served to keep discontented citizens busy.

Thousands, perhaps even millions, of men built the wall, using stone, brick, dirt, or whatever materials happened to be near the section that was being worked on. The wall was actually designed as two walls with packed dirt in between so that a road could be built on top. The construction of the wall was a long and often dangerous process. Many men died during construction, and legends say that thousands of dead laborers lie buried under the wall.

Although much of the Great Wall was erected during the Ch'in period, it was reconstructed during the reign of the dynasties that followed.

The Great Wall of China

A Clay Army

It was common practice among the ancient Chinese as well as other ancient peoples to bury the dead with supplies, such as food, weapons, and money. The Chinese believed in life after death but not as the Bible teaches. Like the Egyptians, they thought that their dead ancestors would live on into the next world, needing those supplies to survive.

In 1974, some Chinese peasants were digging for a well when they made an incredible discovery—an entire clay army keeping a silent guard over the tomb of the emperor Qin Shi Huangdi. Each life-sized statue of this clay army was uniquely carved with great detail, including the weapons in its hands. The clay army included over six thousand soldiers, horses, and chariots and was probably designed to protect the emperor as he lived on into the next world.

Artifacts like this clay army reveal the way people in the ancient world lived and died. One journalist, Audrey Topping, wrote after looking at the clay figures, "Looking into the pit . . . was like looking back more than two thousand years at an ancient battlefield."

Part of the army of life-sized figures found at the tomb of Qin Shi Huangdi

The Han

Compared with other Chinese dynasties, Ch'in rule was very brief. After the Ch'in emperor died, another dynasty, the Han, rose to power around 200 B.C. Replacing the harsh Ch'in, the Han provided a strong, but fair, government.

The Han rulers needed officials to help govern the country. These officials, or *mandarins,* were chosen according to their abilities. A man wanting to be a mandarin had to spend long years studying the Confucian *Classics*. At the end of those years, when he was almost thirty, the candidate had to take some very difficult government tests that involved being locked in a small room for days on end.

If a man passed the upper levels of the test, he was allowed to have the title of a mandarin. A mandarin could be identified by his special robes. He was highly respected for his superior intelligence and education.

The mandarins were not just a group of scholars, however. They were vital to the running of the Chinese government. They supervised government activities that included the building of roads, the dealings of merchants, and the collecting of taxes. Mandarins remained an important part of the Chinese government for more than two thousand years. Today the term *mandarin* refers to a dialect that is spoken by many Chinese people.

The era of the Han proved a glorious period in Chinese history. The Chinese were far ahead of other countries, making progress in writing, medicine, and science. During this period, the first Chinese dictionary was completed with about nine thousand words and their meanings. Included in these early dictionaries were the different ways to write each word.

A common medical treatment was *acupuncture,* a method of relieving pain by sticking needles into certain points of the body. The Chinese also used special herbs as medicine.

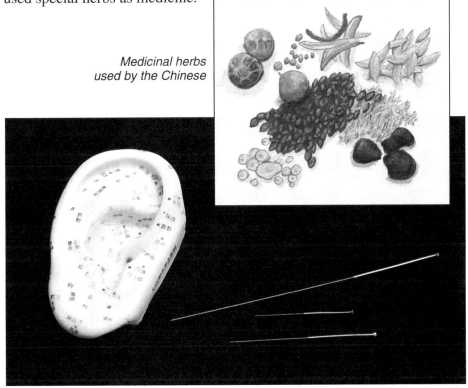

Medicinal herbs used by the Chinese

A model of the ear with acupuncture points labeled (left) and three different sizes of acupuncture needles (right)

The Chinese learned how to mine for salt by using bamboo poles with iron tips. The Chinese would drill thousands of feet underground to get salt water. Then they would use natural gas to heat these mines until the water evaporated, leaving the salt behind. They raised the salt to the surface in bamboo buckets.

One important scientific invention during the Han era was the *seismograph*. Do you know what a seismograph is? It is an instrument that is used to detect and measure earthquakes. The ancient Chinese seismographs were not like the ones that are used today, however. Instead, they were very decorative pieces of bronze.

Look at the pictures on this page. Inside the *urn,* or vase, is a pendulum. Whenever the earth moved, the pendulum would move, hitting a small ball that fell out of the dragon's mouth into the frog's mouth.

The Chinese determined the direction of the earthquake by which frog the ball fell into. Why do you think the ancient Chinese needed a seismograph? Why do we use seismographs today? Earthquakes often cause damage to buildings and land. The Chinese used the bronze seismograph to determine the general location of an earthquake. Then Chinese leaders sent out troops with food and supplies to help people— particularly the farmers, whose work supported the entire country.

Paper

Imagine what our world would be like without paper. We use paper for many things. Can you name a few? Newspapers, textbooks, labels on cans, and money are just a few of the things we use that are made from paper.

Have you ever wondered who were the first people to use paper? The ancient Chinese were. During the Han dynasty, the Chinese made paper by using the hemp plant or the bark from a mulberry tree. They pounded these substances to a pulp and mixed them

Ancient Chinese paper-making process

with water. The mixture was then spread out flat. The dried pulp formed a coarse sheet of paper that was difficult to write on. This early paper was used merely as wrapping for different items or for clothing. Later, the Chinese used rags, rope, or fishing nets to make a smoother pulp.

What did people write on before paper was invented? The ancient Chinese used silk, bone, or turtle shell to keep written records. Other ancient peoples recorded information on clay tablets or on walls. After the Chinese invented paper, they used it to write on and eventually to make paper money. The paper you use today to do your homework is an "echo" of the ancient Chinese invention of paper. Can you think of any advantages or disadvantages of paper compared to the types of surfaces people wrote on earlier?

Rolls of paper being produced in a modern paper factory

115

To Make Paper

1. Help your teacher prepare and set up the equipment for making paper.

2. Listen as your teacher reads the steps needed in making paper.

3. Work with your partner, completing each step as your teacher directs.

The Silk Road

How did Chinese inventions, such as the seismograph or paper, reach other countries? Until the Han dynasty, China had remained a secluded country. Do you remember one reason? Natural barriers had hindered interaction with other peoples. The Han dynasty changed China in many ways. Perhaps one of the most important ways it changed China, and even the rest of the world, was by opening up a trade route that became known as the *Silk Road.*

How do you think the trade route received this name? The Chinese used this route to trade silk and spices for fruits and items that they did not have. The Silk Road crossed many of China's natural barriers, such as mountains and deserts. It stretched for over four thousand miles to the west.

Do you think the people who traded with the Chinese had any influence on China? They brought new products, such as different fruits and even horses from their own lands, to trade with the Chinese. Besides trading products, other countries eventually exchanged ideas and inventions with China.

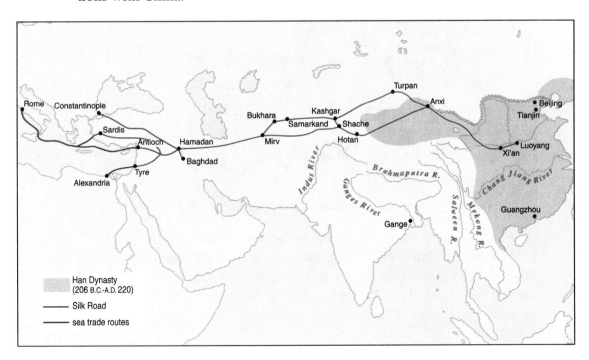

117

The ancient Chinese were a great people. Under the early dynasties, China began to develop and grow, surpassing other countries of the time. The technology of the early Chinese stretches across the centuries to our own day as we use things such as paper and the seismograph.

It is amazing to think that thousands of years ago people secluded from other civilizations were creating inventions that would make our lives easier today. The ancient Chinese laid the foundation for future advances.

Today, traces of China's ancient past may be seen in its culture. The Chinese hold the family as one of the most important aspects of one's life, just as Confucius taught. Education is also important to the modern Chinese as it was centuries ago, and scholars are greatly admired.

Mao Zedong's portrait hangs above the Gate of Heavenly Peace, where he first declared the founding of Communist China in 1949.

Although these values are similar to the ideals held by the ancient Chinese, China's government has greatly changed since the early dynasties in seclusion. Communism strictly rules China, even to the point of limiting families to one child. Today the glory of the ancient Chinese seems dimmed by the reign of Communism. Perhaps someday China will shine once more.

A Glory by the Sea:
Classical Greece

Modern Greek seacoast

The poet Edgar Allan Poe once wrote of "the glory that was Greece." What do you think he meant? Was he describing the land of Greece itself—its steep white rocks towering above a sapphire blue sea? Was he thinking of its architecture—its magnificent marble buildings, its columned porches, its statues? Or was he speaking of the Grecian people, draped in their long, flowing robes or clad in their bronze armor—accomplished warriors, philosophers, mathematicians, poets, and artists?

Poe was clearly referring to the Classical Age of Greece, a period of time beginning about 500 B.C. and lasting nearly two hundred years. Why do we remember these centuries of history in Greece as glorious?

The Classical Age was a peak of human achievement. The culture of the Greeks in this time period made a lasting impact on the Western world. Over the centuries, people have looked back to the classical Greeks for patterns to follow in government, philosophy, and the arts.

The Land and Its People

The homeland of the Greeks was in the same place as the Greece of today. Situated in southern Europe, Greece is a land of mountains, valleys, natural harbors, and hundreds of tiny islands. Greece is a peninsula, bordered by the Ionian Sea on the west, the Mediterranean Sea on the south, and the Aegean Sea on the east. The southern portion of this peninsula is called the *Peloponnesus.*

Because of the mild Mediterranean climate, the Greeks spent much time outdoors. Greece's rugged coastline and island-strewn seas helped make its people seafarers and traders. Often it was easier to go by boat from one place to another than to try to cross the mountains.

Some Greeks were also farmers. The soil in Greece was poor, but farmers could grow crops such as barley, wheat, olives, and grapes. The Greeks often prepared simple meals from these native products even though they imported other types of food.

Greece

Location—Southeastern Europe on the southern end of the Balkan Peninsula.

Climate—Typical Mediterranean climate: long summers and mild, rainy winters. Temperatures range from 80°F in the summer to 48°F in the winter.

Topography—Mountainous with a narrow coastal plain; includes many island groups and the island of Crete.

Natural Resources—Bauxite, iron ore, and small quantities of coal. In 1974 oil was discovered in the Aegean Sea.

Geography and Culture—Greece's mountainous terrain encouraged the growth of independent city-states rather than a unified country.

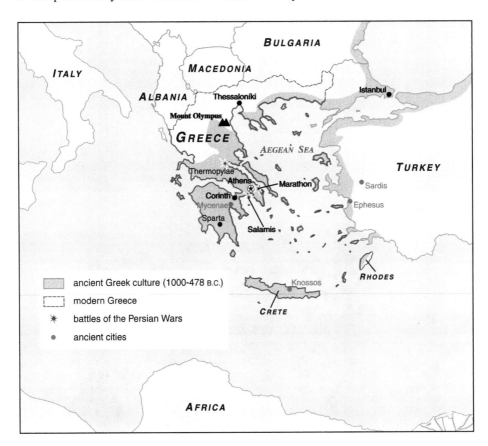

Athens and Sparta

Before the Classical Age of Greece was a period we call the Dark Age. Few records were kept to tell us what life was like in Greece during this time. But we do know a little about how the people lived. How do you think we got this knowledge?

Because Greece's mountains and valleys divided the land, the people lived in independent groups in separate areas. These groups were called *city-states*. The people in a city-state were like a large family—they claimed common ancestors, practiced the same customs, and spoke the same Greek dialect. Rather than having one central government for the entire country, each city-state had its own government. During Greece's Dark Age, most city-states were ruled by a king. The Greeks called this type of government a *monarchy*.

The two most famous city-states were Athens and Sparta. Although they were once similar to one another, they ended up being very different. By the end of the Dark Age, both city-states had adopted a new type of government—an *oligarchy*. By now you might have guessed that the suffix *-archy* means "rule." The prefix *olig-* means "few." Can you guess what *oligarchy* means? It means "rule by the few," and usually the few who rule are the rich upper class.

123

After the Dark Age, many city-states branched out and formed colonies along the Mediterranean Sea. People who had gained wealth and power from trading grew discontent with having an oligarchy ruling over them. Some city-states soon began to form new ideas about what type of government was best. Athens was one of these.

Individual men rose to power in Athens, supported by discontented people. These men were called *tyrants*. Some of them ruled well. Others ruled poorly. Most wanted the lower classes to have better living conditions and more say in government. Several of them passed laws in favor of the lower classes.

By 500 B.C. these laws had greatly changed the government of Athens. Athens became a democracy. The word *democracy* comes from the Greek words meaning "power of the people." Every male citizen over eighteen years old attended meetings of the *Assembly,* listened to leaders speak, and voted. Every male citizen now had a voice in the government of Athens.

The Athenian democracy became the most successful one in the ancient world. Democratic countries today look back to Athens as a model in some ways for government by the people.

Sparta, on the other hand, kept its oligarchy. The oligarchy had one aim—to have a strong army. What do you think life would have been like in a city-state with this goal?

Life in Sparta was much more rigid than life in Athens. For centuries, Sparta made no advances in art or literature as Athens and other city-states did. Such things were forbidden in Sparta. When a baby boy was born, his parents presented him to the rulers of the city. If the rulers thought he was strong, they allowed him to live. If not, they left him in the country-side to die. The Spartans did not want any weaklings in their army. A boy who was not put to death stayed at home until he was seven years old. Then the army took him and trained him to be a soldier.

During most of his young adult life, a Spartan boy lived with a group, or *pack,* of boys. Pack members had little to eat or wear. They were expected to steal food from farms. Every year some of the pack members were beaten in public as part of a ceremony to the gods. At age twenty, a Spartan man was allowed to marry. But he could not live at home with his wife. He had to live with the other men, training to be a soldier, for ten more years. The training a man received in the Spartan army was harsh and disciplined. Why do you think this was true? The Spartans felt that learning to suffer pain and hardship would make a man a good soldier.

What was life like for the women in classical Greece? That depended on where they lived.

Athenian women led sheltered lives. An upper-class woman went out of the house only to festivals and plays and then only when accompanied by servants. Her slaves did the daily shopping and errands. Lower-class women, who did not have slaves, were not as protected, but they rarely shopped or worked outside the home. They stayed home and kept their households supplied with meals and clothing.

Spartan women received physical training much like that of their men. Their training was designed to make them strong mothers. Mothers taught their children to be loyal to the city-state and to uphold Spartan bravery. Women sent their husbands and sons into battle with the cry, "Return with your shield or on it!" Do you know what the women meant? They meant that the soldier should return as a living conqueror or a dead hero. The Spartan army had no room for cowards or quitters.

Women in Greece were not allowed to vote or participate in governmental meetings. But many were thinkers with ideas and talents of their own.

126

War and Restoration

In the fifth century B.C., the Greeks clashed with the mighty Persian Empire. The Persians were angered by the growth of Greek city-states. They wanted to conquer Greece and make it part of their own empire. But they soon found that defeating the Greeks would not be easy. For over ten years the Greeks fought the Persians and had many successes in battle.

In 480 B.C. the Greeks met the forces of Xerxes *(zûrk′sēz)*, the Persian king, at the Battle of Salamis Bay. They burned 200 of the Persians' 350 ships. Following this defeat, the Persians tried only one more time to conquer the Greeks—without success. Greece was victorious.

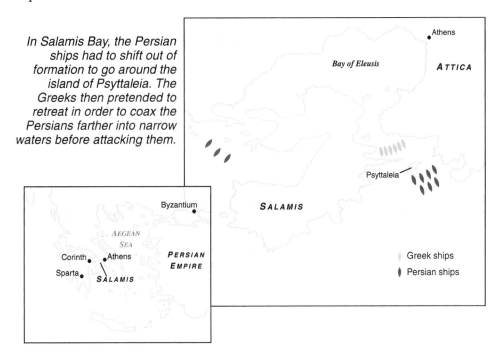

In Salamis Bay, the Persian ships had to shift out of formation to go around the island of Psyttaleia. The Greeks then pretended to retreat in order to coax the Persians farther into narrow waters before attacking them.

Have you ever been a member of a team that beat a stronger rival? If you have, you can probably understand how the Greeks felt after their victory over the Persians. They felt as if they could accomplish anything.

However, war had taken its toll on Greece. Many of the country's buildings and temples lay in ruins. One of the first ways the Greeks put their new confidence to work was in restoring their cities.

Pericles

The most famous leader of the democracy in Athens was Pericles. Pericles is considered one of the greatest public speakers, or *orators,* of all time. The Greeks made him their leader because they respected his wisdom and his ability to reason.

Not only was Pericles a powerful speaker and politician, but he loved the city of Athens as well. He was born and reared in Athens, and he wanted it always to be a city that others would admire and love as he did. After the Persian Wars, he wanted to repair the damages caused when Xerxes burned the city. He wanted to restore to Athens all of its former beauty and more.

The *Acropolis,* a hill overlooking the city, was the center of religious life in Athens. Pericles encouraged the Athenians to rebuild the ruined temple and construct other sacred buildings on that hill. He hired talented architects, sculptors, and artists. Under his leadership Athens, as we remember it, took shape—the columns, the sculptures, the great Entrance Gate. He not only supervised reconstruction of buildings but also supported the growth of manufacturing and trade and helped build up the army.

Pericles so dominated Athens during the fifth century B.C. that this period is often called the *Age of Pericles.*

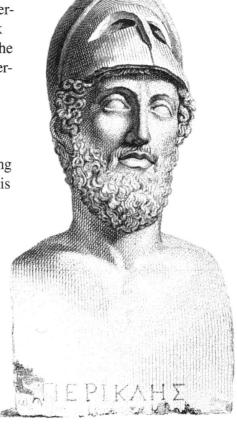

In the center of Athens was the *agora (ăg′ər ə),* a busy marketplace. The agora was made up of open-air buildings called *porches.* Every day, citizens gathered there to buy and sell. Athenians could buy fresh food that had been brought to the agora from local farms. But there was not enough good farmland around Athens to feed all of the people, so some foods, such as meats and cheeses, were imported. Shoppers could also find materials like iron, copper, timber, ivory, animal hides, wool, papyrus, furniture, and textiles.

A modern marketplace in Athens

Food and supplies were not the only things to be found at the agora. Schools, government buildings, courts, and private businesses were located there also. Sometimes people just gathered there, not to shop or conduct business but to discuss politics, philosophy, and the latest news. Would you like to have an agora where you live?

Religion in Classical Greece

The Greeks believed in many different gods. Although they thought that their gods had supernatural powers, they did not believe the gods were much different from humans in other respects. Drawings and sculptures depicted the gods as having human bodies. In their character, too, the gods were like humans—they were jealous, vengeful, immoral, and childish. Do gods like these seem to you to be worthy of reverence?

The Greeks made up stories, called *myths,* about the lives of their gods. You are probably familiar with some of these myths. Have you ever heard the story of Midas, the king with the golden touch? Midas was granted a wish by the god Bacchus. He was told he could have any gift he desired. What would you have asked for? Midas requested that everything he touched might turn to gold. Do you think this was a wise request?

Midas soon came to regret his wish. Every time he tried to eat, his food would turn to gold before he could taste it. Some versions of the story say that he even turned his daughter to a gold statue when he touched her. Eventually, he had to ask Bacchus to take the gift back.

On the Acropolis stands the *Parthenon,* an enormous temple made of white marble surrounded by forty-six columns. This temple is dedicated to Athena, the goddess of wisdom, for whom the city of Athens is named. A huge statue of her once stood in the Parthenon. The statue contained so much ivory and gold and so many jewels that it was worth more than the temple that housed it. Around A.D. 400, the statue was captured by the Romans and taken to Constantinople. Soon afterward it mysteriously disappeared.

The Parthenon is the ultimate example of Greek architecture. Several *optical illusions* have been included in its design. An optical illusion occurs when an object appears to take a shape it does not really have. Have you ever looked down a set of railroad tracks? The rails on each side of the tracks seem to come gradually closer together and meet in the distance. The only way to make the rails appear straight would be to place them farther apart as they get farther away from you.

The architects of the Parthenon created some clever illusions. They distorted their work on purpose to correct appearance problems. The steps leading up to the temple are humped in the center, but they appear perfectly level from a distance. The columns lean slightly inward and are thicker in the middle than at the top and base. But to the eye they appear straight and tall.

The Parthenon as it might have appeared in ancient times

The Parthenon

Parthenon ruins as they appear today

The Parthenon has been used in many different ways since it was first constructed by the Greeks over two thousand years ago. For many years it was a pagan temple dedicated to Athena. It is now believed to have been a place of human sacrifice. No one knows exactly what it looked like at that time. It was carved with designs and sculptures that told stories about the lives of Athena and the other gods.

In the Middle Ages, the Parthenon was used as a church. Christians met there, and the walls must have echoed with the notes of their hymns. Later, after Turkish Muslim forces captured Athens, the Parthenon became a Muslim mosque. The walls heard different echoes then—the hollow sounds of muttered prayers to Allah.

While the Turks ruled Athens, they stored gunpowder and ammunition in the Parthenon. During a battle with the Venetians in 1687, a shot landed in the Parthenon and set off an explosion. The building is now only an empty shell, but thousands of tourists travel to Athens each year to admire it. They can still see in its remains the beauty and intricacy of its architecture. Perhaps, too, they like to imagine they can hear "echoes" of voices that spoke there when it was the beautiful Greek temple of long ago.

Knowledge in Classical Greece

Would you like to go to school with a servant who was there just to make sure you behaved? Wealthy boys in Greece had to do this. The servants who accompanied them were called pedagogues. Boys began school at age six and continued at least to age fourteen. At school they studied reading, writing, arithmetic, grammar, music, and sports. Boys from poorer families could not afford to go to school, and girls were not allowed to go at all.

Reading was much different in classical Greece from how it is at your school. The Greeks had an alphabet with only twenty-four letters. Some letters were the same as ours, and some were different. The Greeks used no punctuation or spacing between words.

Writing was different as well. Greek students wrote on wax-coated tablets with an instrument called a *stylus*. The stylus was pointed on one end to scratch letters into the wax and blunt on the other end to rub out mistakes.

The Greeks used a special instrument called an *abacus* to teach math. Perhaps you have seen one. It is a wooden frame with rows of movable beads on it.

Playing the aulos

Do you take music lessons? The Greeks regarded music as the greatest of all the arts, more important than architecture, painting, sculpture, or literature. The Greek god Apollo was believed to be the god of music. Greek art often pictures Apollo entertaining the other gods with a *lyre,* or small harp, in his hands. The Greeks also believed that a group of nine goddesses called *the Muses* presided over the arts. Each goddess had a particular specialty, such as epic poetry or religious music. Can you guess where our word *music* comes from?

If you were a wealthy boy in classical Greece, you would be required to study music but probably not the type you are used to. Greek students learned to play the lyre and the *aulos (ou′läs),* a type of flute.

Singing was also an important part of a Greek boy's musical training. Students memorized the *Iliad* and the *Odyssey,* two great works by the poet Homer, who lived during the Greek Dark Age. Instead of reciting these lengthy poems, the students put them to music and sang them. Some boys continued their studies with training in public speaking, hoping to become leaders in the democracy.

The Greeks believed that developing the body was as important as developing the mind. Our English word *athlete* comes from the Greek language. Schoolboys spent hours in the gymnasium running, jumping, wrestling, boxing, and throwing the javelin and the discus.

The Greeks held special festivals in which athletes took part. These festivals were held in honor of the gods. Athletes from all over Greece would travel to the city where the festival was being held to compete in various events. Does this sound familiar? What festival of games still takes place in our modern world?

The Greeks were the first to hold the Olympic Games. The games were held at the city of Olympia. Athletes competed in many of the same events as do athletes of today—sprints, long jumps, discus and javelin throwing, and wrestling. They also had chariot races and events for younger boys. The winners were given garlands of olive leaves to wear on their heads as crowns.

Do you know what the word *philosopher* means? It means "lover of wisdom." During the Classical Age of Greece, many thoughtful scholars lived in Athens. These men were called *philosophers.*

Socrates *(sŏk′rə tēz′)* taught by asking his students thought-provoking questions. "What is the meaning of life?" he would ask. "What is a good man?" The questions made his students think about what they really believed. How would you answer these questions? Socrates was also a firm believer in democracy, but he wanted to make the government a perfect one. He believed that right thinking would lead to right actions.

Plato was one of Socrates' students. Plato wrote books in the form of conversations. In these books, called *dialogues,* he said that the ideal government was ruled by a few of the most intelligent men. He also taught that there was a *spiritual world*—a world of the mind and of ideas—that was superior to the physical world.

Aristotle *(ăr′ĭ stŏt′l),* Plato's pupil, was a third great philosopher. Science, to him, was the most important academic subject. We give him credit for the *scientific method,* a method of study requiring careful observation and record keeping. He also taught that reason controls behavior.

School of Athens, *Raphael's famous painting in the Vatican, depicts Plato and Aristotle (center back) with other Greek scientists and philosophers around them.*

Not only philosophers but also other learned men lived in Greece. When you study math and certain types of science, you rely upon the discoveries of several Greek scholars. Archimedes *(är′kə mē′dēz)* was a mathematician who perfected the lever and compound pulleys, machines that make the moving of objects easier. Euclid wrote the first geometry book. The entire study of geometry was built around his teachings. Pythagoras *(pĭ thăg′ər·əs),* another mathematician, studied geometry and came up with an important *theorem,* or carefully tested idea, about triangles.

Pythagoras

Look at a map of the world. Did you know that a Greek named Eratosthenes *(ĕr′ə tŏs′thə·nēz)* was the first to draw the latitude and longitude lines on the map? He also calculated the circumference of the earth with reasonable accuracy.

An astronomer named Aristarchus *(ăr′ĭ stär′kəs)* was the first to suggest that the universe was sun centered rather than earth centered, as most people of those days believed.

Two other Greeks, Hippocrates *(hĭ pŏk′rə tēz′)* and Herodotus, *(hĭ rŏd′ə təs)* are famous today for their contributions. Hippocrates, called the Father of Medicine, did not agree with the idea of relying on magic to treat patients. He examined them carefully and prescribed treatment. Doctors today still take the Hippocratic Oath in honor of this man's wisdom and principles in the medical profession. Herodotus is called the Father of History. Much of what we know about life in classical Greece comes from the careful notes that he recorded during that time.

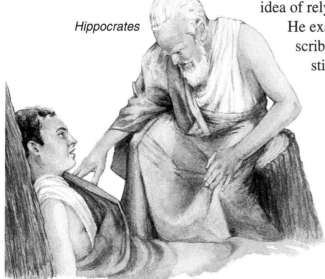

Hippocrates

Art in Classical Greece

Greek artists wanted their work to be perfect. They strove to create the ideal representation of an object or person. Important qualities of Greek art were balance, completeness, harmony, simplicity, and beauty.

Much of what we know about how the Greeks lived and dressed comes from their art. The work of painters adorned plates, jugs, pots, jars, cups, bowls, and perfume bottles. Metal craftsmen decorated gold and silver cups and fashioned delicate jewelry. Sculptors' work appeared in marble statues and on coins. In wall murals, floor mosaics, and embroidery, Greek art flourished as well. Many artists portrayed human beings or gods and goddesses. Others depicted mythological creatures such as Pegasus, the winged horse, or animals and birds, such as goats, deer, bulls, lions, dolphins, and cranes.

Greek grave relief, 450-440 B.C.

The Metropolitan Museum of Art, Fletcher Fund, 1927

Photograph © 1997 The Metropolitan Museum of Art

Athenian jar, ca. 540 B.C.

The Metropolitan Museum of Art, Rogers Fund, 1917 (17.230.14a,b); Gift of J.D. Beazley, 1927 (27.16)

Photograph © 1999 The Metropolitan Museum of Art

Greek architecture, too, expresses the Greek love of beauty and harmony. Compare a Greek temple with an Egyptian pyramid or a Sumerian ziggurat. What differences do you see?

Compare the pyramid of Khafra in Egypt to Greek temples.

Greek Erechtheum (Porch of the Maidens), Acropolis, Athens

The Greeks perfected another art form as well—the art of drama. Crowds would gather in huge outdoor theaters called *amphitheaters* to watch the actors perform plays as part of religious festivals.

Most Greek plays were about gods and heroes. There were two types of Greek drama: *comedy* and *tragedy*. Comedies were meant to make the audience laugh and to put them in a lighthearted mood. Tragedies were meant to instruct. They usually ended with the downfall of the hero because of some character flaw, such as pride or jealousy. Tragedies left audiences feeling more sober. They often made people think about themselves and their failures. Which type of drama would you have preferred?

A modern Greek mask play

An ancient Greek dramatic mask

Greek plays were very different from the plays we are used to today. Imagine that you are sitting on a cool stone bench in a large amphitheater in ancient Greece, far away from the stage. How could you hear the actors' voices and see the expressions on their faces? You would probably have very little trouble because the actors would be wearing exaggerated costumes and large masks that would allow you to tell them apart. Some of them might exchange their masks for different ones when they were happy or sad or angry. The funnel-shaped mouthpieces inside the masks acted as megaphones that made actors' voices carry to everyone in the crowd.

To Make a Greek Mask

1. Decide what character quality or emotion you want to represent with your mask.

2. Practice several emotions as you hold a mirror in front of your face. Note the facial distinctions for each emotion.

3. Draw a face on construction paper, trying to show the quality or emotion you chose in Step 1.

4. Cut out holes for the eyes.

5. Hold your mask in front of your face, and allow the other students to guess what emotion you tried to illustrate.

The Spread of Greek Culture

In 431 B.C., a war began that was to change Greece forever. Following the Persian Wars, some of the city-states had joined with Athens in a league for protection from the Persians. Sparta and its allies began to see Athens and its allies as a threat, and soon war broke out between the two groups. This war was called the Peloponnesian War, and it lasted twenty-seven years. Who do you think won in the end?

Sparta, with its well-trained warriors, won the war. But it proved to be weak in ruling the democratic city-states it had conquered. Quarrels broke out between city-states. The weakened condition of Greece allowed Philip II of Macedonia to take control of its government in 338 B.C.

Philip died two years later, and his son Alexander took the throne of Macedonia. Alexander had been tutored by Aristotle, and he loved the Greek ways of life and philosophy. He took control of the army at the age of twenty and began to pursue his dream of uniting the entire world under one empire. He extended his rule eastward as far as India, spreading the Greek culture through much of the world. His military genius and unconquerable spirit have earned him the title "Alexander the Great."

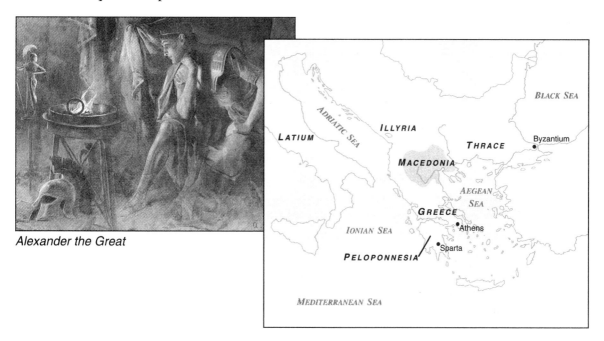

Alexander the Great

Now people all over the Western world were becoming like the Greeks. They adopted the ideas of Greek philosophers. They used Greek inventions and learned the teachings of Greek scholars. The works of Greek artists appeared in all parts of the empire.

Most importantly, the spread of Greek culture brought a common language to the Western world. The Greek language was now the official language for all of Alexander's empire. It was understood by both the commoner and the nobleman. What were some advantages of having a common language?

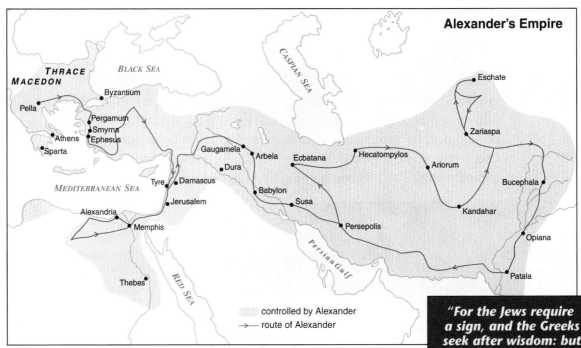

Alexander's Empire

controlled by Alexander
→ route of Alexander

The Greek language made communication throughout the empire much easier. Imagine the possibilities. People could travel for miles and still meet others who spoke their language. The written word could be read and understood throughout the region. In a few centuries, there would be a very important message to carry to the world—the message of Jesus Christ. The spread of the Greek language paved the way for the gospel to go into all the world.

"For the Jews require a sign, and the Greeks seek after wisdom: but we preach Christ crucified, unto the Jews a stumblingblock, and unto the Greeks foolishness; but unto them which are called, both Jews and Greeks, Christ the power of God, and the wisdom of God."

I Corinthians 1:22-24

Paul's Sermon on Mars' Hill

The Classical Greeks were some of the most well-educated, artistic, and talented people of all time. In the eyes of most of the world, the Greeks had everything. They were a successful people. But can you think of one important thing that was missing from their lives?

After Christ's work on earth was finished, Paul was called to be a missionary. He was called to the Jews first and then to the Greeks. During his travels, he spent some time in the city of Athens. Acts 17 tells us that one of the first things he noticed about the city was its widespread idolatry. The Greeks may have possessed knowledge of many different subjects, but they had no knowledge of God.

As Paul walked through the city, he found an altar with an inscription carved into it. "To the Unknown God," it read. When he stood up to speak to the Athenians on Mars' Hill, he told them about the one true God. He told them that God is not a statue made of gold or silver and not a name carved in stone. He is real, He is Creator and Lord, and He wants people everywhere to repent and seek Him.

Do you think the Athenians believed? Many made fun of Paul's message. Some left thoughtfully, wanting to hear more. But a few men and women grasped the truth of Paul's words and believed with all their hearts. Paul's mission trip to Athens had not been in vain.

View of the Acropolis from Mars Hill

The glory of Greece could not last forever. After Alexander's death, his empire was divided into four parts. Most of this empire would later be conquered by Rome.

We owe a great deal to the Greeks. Look around you. Every time you see a column, you are seeing an example of Greek architecture. Every time you watch a play, you are enjoying the contributions the Greeks made to drama. Every time you admire a sculpture or read a lovely poem, you are appreciating the very arts that the Greeks perfected. And when you study literature, science, math, and history, you are reaping the benefits of Greek discoveries in those realms.

Open your Bible to the New Testament. Every word you see on all the pages was originally written in the Greek language. Aren't you glad that the Greeks had an alphabet and writing skills? The richness of their language gave us a detailed history of the Lord Jesus Christ and helped point the way to heaven.

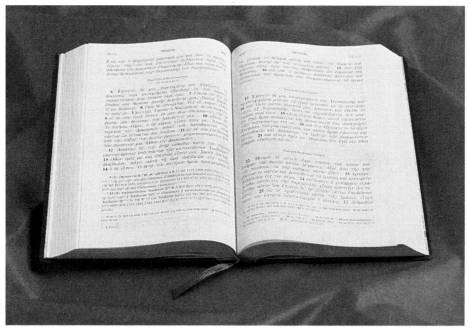

A New Testament in the Greek language

Power of the Seven Hills:
Roman World

Long ago, in the land we now call Italy, twin brothers were born. Abandoned by their mother, they were left floating in a basket on the Tiber River. A wolf spied the basket from the shore and swam out into the river to investigate. Tiny cries came from inside the little vessel. The wolf dragged the basket to the safety of the shore and waited for help to come.

Soon a shepherd wandered by and found the two babies crying in the basket. "What is this?" he asked himself. "Orphans, no doubt. I will take them home with me."

The shepherd and his wife named the twin brothers Romulus and Remus. They reared them to be brave young men. When they were grown, the brothers decided to build a city on the Tiber River so that they would remember the place of their rescue.

But they could not agree on the exact spot. Romulus wanted to build on the seven hills near the river's mouth. Remus began marking out different boundaries. In anger, Romulus killed his brother, buried him, and built the city of Rome on top of Remus's grave. Later, as the ruler of Rome, he kept an empty throne next to his, in memory of Remus.

Do you believe that this story is true? It is a popular legend about the founding of the city of Rome.

Rome: The City

Rome has been a city, a republic, and an empire. Now it is once again a city in Italy. Rome began around 753 B.C. when a group of settlers from central Europe called *Latins* made their homes there. The Latins were farmers and herdsmen, and Rome was their city.

The Latins had been living in Rome for over one hundred years when another tribe, the *Etruscans,* conquered them. The Etruscans were from northern Italy, and their culture had been influenced by the Greeks. They were skilled at trading and architecture. The Etruscan kings were powerful, and Rome became the most respected city in the region. But the Latins did not like having the Etruscan kings ruling over them.

In 509 B.C., the nobles of the city drove the Etruscan king, Tarquin the Proud, from the throne. Rome no longer had kings. The republic of Rome had begun. From then on the Latins were known as *Romans.*

An Etruscan bronze sculpture of a warrior

Italy

Location—A boot-shaped peninsula in southern Europe, including Sardinia, Sicily, and a number of other smaller islands.

Climate—Temperate in the north, except for the cooler mountain regions; milder in the south. The average temperature ranges from 33°F to 70°F.

Topography—Mountainous, including the Apennine range and sections of the Alps, but also has broad plains. Most of its islands are mountainous.

Natural Resources—Natural gas, hydroelectric power, rich soil, and small quantities of sulfur and mercury.

Geography and Culture—Being surrounded by water made Italy's people seafarers. Italy's central location in the Mediterranean Sea enabled the Romans to be one of the first peoples to establish a vast empire.

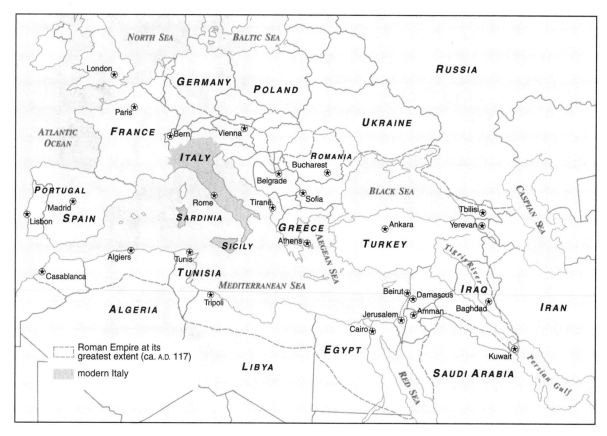

Rome: The Republic

Do you know what the word *republic* means? It comes from the Latin words that mean "belonging to the people." In a republic, the government is the people's responsibility.

In Rome, the citizens elected representatives to pass laws for all of Rome. But not everyone in Rome could vote at first. Only *patricians,* or members of the noble class, could vote. The common workers, small farmers, artisans, merchants, and foreigners were called *plebeians,* and they did not have the privilege of voting. Do you think everyone in Rome was satisfied with this arrangement?

The plebeians protested, and they were finally allowed to have their own governing body. It was called the *Assembly,* and their leaders were called *tribunes*. The patricians' body was the Senate, governed by *consuls*. The Assembly could not make official laws, but the Senate could. One of the first things the Assembly asked the Senate to do was to write down the law. The members of the Senate had the Roman law engraved on twelve bronze tablets and set into the temple wall where everyone could see it.

In this painting, the artist Macarra showed the Roman Senate as it might have looked in ancient times.

The plebeians were also given *veto power.* The Latin word *veto* means "I forbid." Tribunes stood in the Senate doorway during its meetings. The tribunes could stop the Senate's actions at any time by shouting, "Veto!"

Gradually, the plebeians gained more rights. They were allowed to marry patricians. They could be elected as consuls. At last, the Assembly was permitted to make laws that were just as official as those the Senate made. The plebeians and the patricians now had equal say in the government of Rome.

Would you expect a republic like this one to work? It worked very well for several hundred years. Most people in Rome worked hard and respected the law. And most lawmakers wanted to help and protect the citizens of Rome.

The Roman Republic Worked

1. Find out from your teacher whether you will be a member of the Senate or of the Assembly.

2. Go to your appropriate place and follow the instructions as the meeting proceeds.

3. Discuss the meeting with your classmates. Did you feel as if your opinion was important? Was your decision respected by the other group? Do you think this method of making laws is a good one?

What protects a republic? One factor that gave Rome strength was its military forces. Roman soldiers were disciplined and well trained. Rome's infantry was divided into *legions,* units of several thousand men. The soldiers in these units were called *legionaries.*

You have probably seen pictures of Roman legionaries in artists' portrayals of the crucifixion of Christ. These soldiers wore short wool tunics under leather jackets reinforced with metal strips. Bronze helmets protected all but their ears and faces. Centurions and other officers wore tall crests on top of their helmets so that they could be seen easily. Each legionary carried a short sword and a six-foot javelin that weighed about ten pounds.

In the early years of the republic, Rome's legions conquered the entire Italian peninsula. With all of Italy under its control, Rome turned next to the west. Over the next 125 years, Rome battled the North African city of Carthage for control of the Mediterranean Sea. The three major wars between Rome and Carthage are called the *Punic Wars.*

The Second Punic War

The Second Punic War is the most famous of the three wars because of a man named Hannibal. Hannibal was the general of the armies of Carthage and a brilliant soldier. He decided that, in order to defeat Rome, he would first invade Italy and win the support of the other Italian peoples against the Romans. He gathered his army in Spain. To avoid having the Romans see him, he planned to march his soldiers eastward into Italy across the cold, rugged Alps.

Hannibal left Spain with about forty thousand men and a group of war elephants. Elephants were often effective in ancient warfare. Enemy lines would break in fear when elephants charged them, and horses shied away from them because they disliked their smell. But Hannibal never got a chance to use his elephants against the Romans. The cold weather was hard on the elephants, and most of them died in the snowy Alps. Many of Hannibal's soldiers did not survive the journey either.

By the time Hannibal's army reached Italy, it was much smaller than the Roman army. But Hannibal's skill at planning strategies made up for the size of his army. He won battle after battle against the Romans. But he could not completely defeat them.

Finally, Rome's Senate found a commander who was equal in ability to Hannibal. This new general, Scipio, decided to win the war by ignoring Hannibal. He and his army left Italy and attacked Carthage. Hannibal immediately rushed home to protect his city. The battle that followed was hard fought, but Scipio gained the victory. Hannibal fled and committed suicide rather than die at the hands of Rome. Carthage made peace with Rome, and the Second Punic War ended.

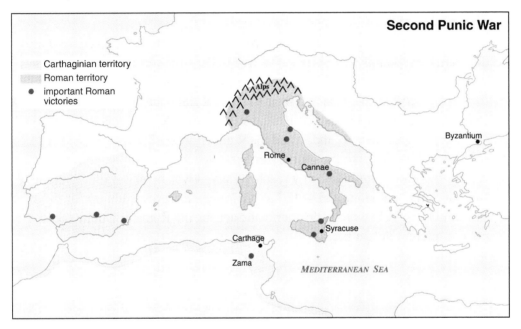

While fighting Carthage, Romans conquered other lands. They marched eastward and conquered the remnants of Alexander the Great's empire. Then they conquered Greece itself and gained control over the eastern Mediterranean Sea. The great sea was now a Roman lake.

When the soldiers returned home, they discovered that more than just Rome's boundaries had changed. Citizen farmers who had left their farms to be soldiers now lost their property. They moved to the city to find work. But most jobs had already been filled by slaves taken from conquered territories. The rich class took advantage of the poor by buying their votes and filling the government with other rich men. How long would you expect this kind of republic to last?

Building Roads

Have you ever heard the saying, "All roads lead to Rome"? Rome is famous for the system of roads it built to connect the lands it had conquered.

Many goods were taken along the Roman roads to other lands. Money, grain, slaves, and precious metals traveled back into Rome as *tribute,* or taxes paid to a ruler by conquered peoples.

Ideas also traveled along the roads. Visitors to Rome carried Roman philosophies away with them. Rome also borrowed knowledge from other lands. The Romans used and improved on the inventions and discoveries of others. They adopted religions from faraway places. Cultures from the East and the West blended, and each changed.

Eventually, the Romans learned how to cut through mountains and keep the roads straight. Roman roads were fast and easy to travel. After five hundred years of building roads to every part of its empire, Rome had a road system with a combined length of ten times the circumference of the earth.

The Roman road on the right had stepping stones placed so that people could cross on them and chariot wheels could go between them.

The Collapse of the Republic

As the plebeians of Rome gave up their right to rule, they became less and less concerned about how the government was run. They no longer studied the issues so that they could vote carefully. They cared only that the government fed and protected them.

Violence became common in Rome. Different men tried to rise to power with the support of the common people. Civil wars broke out between different leaders and their followers.

In 100 B.C., a child was born who would grow up to bring dramatic changes to the government of Rome. Julius Caesar was born in the month later named for him, July.

Roman statue of Julius Caesar

As a member of a patrician family in Rome, Julius Caesar received an excellent education in his youth. He married a patrician and was quick to make his voice heard in government. He had an eloquence and determination that made him popular with the people, and he rose early to high positions in the government.

He was also an outstanding military general. Leading a mighty army of fifty thousand men, he began conquering the land northwest of Italy, called Gaul. For nine years his soldiers defeated tribes in what is today Switzerland, France, Spain, Holland, Belgium, and parts of Germany. Caesar even attacked Britain, which until then had been an unknown land.

Caesar's next conquest came in Rome itself. His popularity as a conqueror threatened the power of the government leaders. The Senate ordered Caesar to disband his army and return to Rome. However, at the Rubicon River, Caesar made his decision to disobey and to return to Rome with his army. This action immediately plunged him into a civil war against the strongest Roman leader, Pompey. Caesar fought Pompey's army for four years before defeating it.

Roman bust of Pompey

In 46 B.C., the Senate proclaimed Caesar dictator of Rome. At first his term was to last only ten years, but he soon changed it so that he would be dictator for life. He made many changes in the government, hoping to solve the problems of the republic.

He limited the power of the corrupt Senate. He granted citizenship to people from Italian territories and even allowed them to have members in the Senate. He promoted colonization, schools, libraries, and public works in all of Rome and its surrounding territories. His actions helped to unify Rome and strengthen its bonds with its conquered peoples.

How do you think the Romans felt about Caesar's methods of governing Rome? Although many Romans liked Caesar and respected his accomplishments, many others were angry with him. They knew that as long as Caesar insisted on having absolute power, the government of Rome could be a true republic no longer.

Julius Caesar's Calendar

Have you ever wondered where the leap year got its start? Julius Caesar originated it when he was ruler of Rome.

One of the biggest problems facing Julius Caesar when he came to power was the calendar. In the past, Roman calendars had ignored the fact that the solar year lasts not just 365 days, but $365\frac{1}{4}$ days. By the time of Caesar's reign, the calendar was so far off that none of the seasons fell in the right place. Caesar had the idea to add an extra day every four years to balance out the calendar. The fourth year is called a leap year, and the extra day is added to February.

Before putting his new idea into practice, Caesar had to bring the calendar up-to-date. So, Caesar made the year 46 B.C. last 445 days! This extra-long year was often called the "year of confusion."

I don't care WHAT month you think it SHOULD be, Aras! If we don't all cooperate, we'll NEVER get this calendar thing straightened out!

Caesar's calendar, known as the Julian calendar, was used by Europeans for centuries. Today we use a reformed version of this calendar, called the *Gregorian calendar.* But "echoes" of Caesar's calendar can still be heard in the names of our months. Many of the months were named after Roman gods or rulers.

The Ides of March

As Caesar's reign continued, angry Romans grew more and more desperate. They wanted the government of Rome to "belong to the people" again. Brutus and Cassius, two senators whom Caesar had considered his friends, met with a group of other Senate members. Secretly they plotted to kill Caesar.

On the fifteenth day of March, called the *ides* of March on the Roman calendar, these men hid in the Senate chamber with knives. When Caesar entered the room, they attacked him and stabbed him. Caesar fell dead at the foot of a statue of Pompey, his old enemy.

Do you think killing Caesar solved the problems of the republic? These senators had broken the law in trying to uphold the law. Their actions had weakened the laws of the republic. And now many other men were eager to take Caesar's place as ruler of Rome. From that time on, men, and not laws, would rule Rome.

Julius Caesar stabbed by Brutus in a scene from Shakespeare's Julius Caesar *(Bob Jones University Classic Players)*

Cicero

Marcus Tullius Cicero was a member of the Roman Senate and a famous orator. He composed over one hundred speeches, all of them known for their exact language, creative descriptions, and clear statements of his ideas.

Cicero was born into a middle-class family of Arpinum, Italy, and received a good education. He studied *rhetoric* (persuasive language), philosophy, and Greek and Latin literature. He became an expert in the Latin language. He even thought of Latin words for technical Greek phrases and ideas.

Cicero became famous as a defense lawyer in Rome. In 63 B.C., he was chosen for the office of consul, Rome's highest elected position. That same year he spared Rome from a military takeover by Lucius Catiline, who wanted to establish a dictatorship.

Cicero was killed by Mark Antony in 43 B.C. because he opposed the heavy government control that Antony wanted to force on Rome. Yet Cicero is still remembered today as one of Rome's greatest patriots, a man who represented the true spirit of its republic.

Rome: The Empire

Caesar's death paved the way for the beginning of Rome's history as an empire. Rome had already conquered many territories and was technically an empire at the time of Caesar. But Rome's new leader, Octavian, was the first to hold the title *imperator,* from which we get our words *empire* and *emperor.*

Octavian, Julius Caesar's adopted son, came to power around 30 B.C., after a fifteen-year struggle with his rivals. He worked to restore honesty, diligence, and respect to the government of Rome. He restored power to the Senate and Tribal Assembly, reserving the office of tribune for himself. He could propose or veto new laws. He also reorganized the army and the governments of Rome's territories. He continued to promote trade and industry and to build roads throughout the empire.

Octavian had complete control of Rome, but he did not call himself a dictator as Caesar had done. He called himself by several different titles. One of these was *Princeps,* meaning "first citizen." Another was *Augustus,* or "revered one." Would you say that he lived up to this title?

Octavian's reign began a period of peace and prosperity that Rome enjoyed for the next two hundred years. This period is called *Pax Romana,* which means "Peace of Rome."

During the Pax Romana, Roman culture was similar to Greek culture in many ways. Like the Greeks, the Romans placed importance on learning, architecture, and religion.

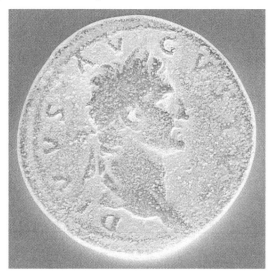

This Roman coin displays the image of Augustus Caesar.

Learning in the Pax Romana

During the republic, children had been reared by their mothers. But during the empire period, many wealthy families left this job to *pedagogues*. Both boys and girls received an education outside the home. They studied reading, writing, and mathematics. After mastering these basics, most girls stayed home to learn the art of homemaking, but some studied further with a private tutor.

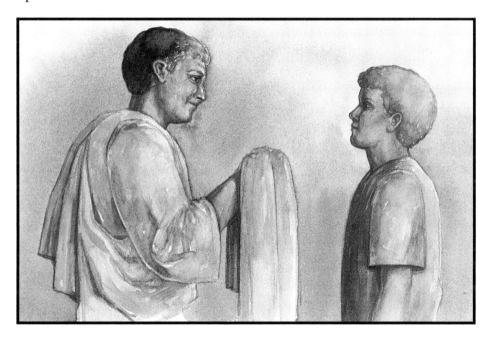

Boys continued their education by studying Greek, Latin, history, geography, astronomy, and literature. At sixteen a boy became a citizen, and a special citizenship ceremony was held at the *Forum,* the Roman marketplace. The boy was given an official citizen's garment—a loose, one-piece robe called a *toga.* He was also given a man's haircut and his first shave.

After becoming citizens, young men continued their studies or entered business or the army. Many Roman adults read a great deal. Some of Rome's best writers lived during Octavian's reign. Virgil wrote the *Aeneid,* an epic about the founding of Rome. Livy wrote a detailed history of Rome, including events from the day in which he lived.

Architecture in the Pax Romana

Rome's greatest artistic achievements were in architecture. The Romans built for practical purposes rather than beauty, but their works are impressive. Before Octavian died, he claimed that he had found Rome as a city of brick and left it as a city of marble.

Romans were the first to use *concrete,* a mixture of gravel and sand in mortar. Rather than build in solid marble, Romans often built in concrete and covered the structure with a thin layer of marble. Not only did concrete help lower building costs, but it also made Roman structures so durable that many still exist today.

A Roman aqueduct in modern Turkey

After the fall of Rome, the process of making concrete was lost for many centuries. A British engineer rediscovered it in the 1700s. Concrete is widely used today. The sidewalks in your neighborhood are probably made of concrete. What other concrete structures are near you?

The Romans borrowed the idea of the *arch* from the Sumerians. Arches enhance most Roman structures, including temples, houses, and even *aqueducts,* raised troughs that carried water through the city. Sometimes the Romans put several arches back-to-back to make a tunnel called a *barrel vault.* And they were the first to put several arches together to make a *dome.* The largest domed building in Rome was a temple called the *Pantheon.* It still stands in Rome today, with a dome rising fourteen stories high.

A painting by Giovanni Paolo of the interior of the Pantheon

Religion in the Pax Romana

Like the Greeks, the Romans worshiped many gods. The Roman religion included many of the Greek gods, but the Romans called them by different names. The Romans worshiped with many rituals, offerings, and prayers.

To the Romans, an emperor was like a god. The Romans used the term *Augustus* for their gods, but every emperor during the time of the empire also carried this title. Some emperors demanded that the Roman people worship them.

The Romans accepted other religions from different parts of their empire. Religions from the Far East became popular.

Apollo, Roman god of prophecy, music, medicine, and poetry

Two Greek philosophies were also practiced as religions in Rome. *Epicureanism* was a belief that there is no God, that no life after death exists, and that the present is all that matters. Epicureans lived for pleasure alone and tried to keep their lives happy and free from pain. A very different Greek philosophy was called *Stoicism*. The Stoics believed that duty was all that mattered in life, and they emphasized bravery in battle and obeying laws. Stoicism was popular among the Roman soldiers.

Diana, Apollo's twin, Roman goddess of hunting and childbirth

165

Christ in the Roman World

> *"But when the fulness of the time was come, God sent forth his Son, made of a woman, made under the law."*
>
> **Galatians 4:4**

What would you say is the most important event in all of human history? That question has only one true answer. The most important event took place during the Pax Romana. Christ was born into the world, lived, and died for the sins of all mankind.

God chose the Pax Romana as His perfect time for Jesus Christ to live on earth. His birth in Bethlehem instead of Joseph's home city of Nazareth was the result of Caesar Augustus's decree that everyone in the Roman Empire return to his birthplace to be taxed. God used this decree to fulfill the prophecy in Micah 5:2 that the Messiah would be born in Bethlehem.

During his life, Christ supported the Roman government by paying the required tax to Caesar. He encouraged the other Jews to do the same (Matthew 22:21).

The method of Christ's death reflected the era in which He lived. After His trials, he was condemned to death by crucifixion, a typical Roman means of execution. In this way God fulfilled Christ's words that the Messiah would be "lifted up" in death (John 12:32) and the Old Testament prophecy that none of His bones would be broken (Psalm 34:20).

Il Sodoma, Procession to Calvary, *The Bob Jones University Collection*

After Christ's death, His followers throughout the Roman Empire were hated. One Roman emperor, Nero, blamed the Christians for starting a fire that destroyed nearly two-thirds of the city of Rome. Without enough evidence to convict them, he ordered many Christians to be put to death by crucifixion or burning.

Through the empire's remaining years, the Romans continued to persecute and torture Christians in cruel ways. Because there was not enough work for everyone in Rome, the people had plenty of time for leisure activities, such as feasts, circuses, and the theater. Another favorite pastime was held in large arenas, such as the Colosseum. There Roman citizens would watch men called gladiators fight other men or animals to the death. During the reign of the emperor Diocletian, Christians, rather than *gladiators,* were released into the arena to be killed by lions.

Do you think these persecutions caused Christians to give up their faith? The Christians became even more determined to follow Christ when they saw the courage of others. They held secret worship services in underground tombs called *catacombs* and spoke out boldly when questioned about their faith in Christ.

> "Blessed are ye, when men shall revile you, and persecute you, and shall say all manner of evil against you falsely, for my sake. Rejoice, and be exceeding glad: for great is your reward in heaven: for so persecuted they the prophets which were before you."
>
> **Matthew 5:11-12**

Colosseum

Catacombs

In A.D. 286, Diocletian decided that the Roman Empire was too large to be ruled by one man. He divided the empire in half, keeping the eastern part under his own control and appointing another ruler for the western part. He eventually appointed assistant rulers for each half, further dividing his power.

Later in Diocletian's reign, a struggle for power began and turned into civil war in the empire. The Pax Romana was only a memory. Soon the Roman Empire itself would collapse and fall to invading tribes from the north.

We remember Greece for its glory—its beautiful artwork, its elegant poetry, its athletic grace. But how do we remember the civilization of Rome? We uphold Rome for its practicality and its power. Massive domes, arched aqueducts, grand road systems, brave legionaries, and fiery patriots who lived and died for the republic— these are the things we think of when we remember Rome.

Of Jade and Stone:
Ancient Mayas

The Other Side of the World

Thousands of miles from Rome and Greece, there lived a people in what is now part of Mexico and Central America. They were accomplished artists, mathematicians, and builders. Their huge civilization was a secret from Europe until Columbus met one of their sailors on his voyage to the Americas. Even then, it was years before a European saw their cities. They were the Mayas, the dominant culture in the ancient Americas.

Mayan Inventions

Is there a zero in your telephone number or your street address? The ancient Mayas developed the idea of zero, an abstract idea that even the Greeks and Romans did not know about. The Babylonians and the Hindus of India also invented a zero, but the Europeans did not use the number until hundreds of years later. With their zero, the Mayas were able to do difficult calculations and keep detailed records.

Mayan Numbers 0–20

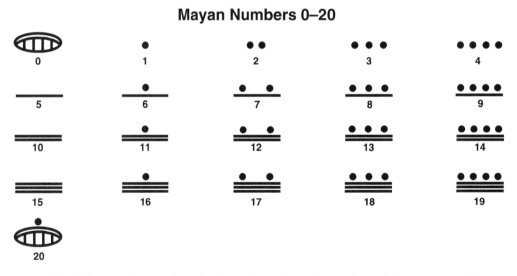

The Mayas also made calendars based on the cycles of the moon and the sun. Their solar year had the same number of days that ours does. The Mayas made their calendars after years of careful sky watching. Their observations were so accurate that they figured out the orbits of the planets and could predict an eclipse of the sun.

The Desire for Chocolate

Do you like hot chocolate? Many people do. It is a tasty "echo" from the tables of Mayan kings and noblemen. The Mayas invented the drink that, with some variations, has been popular for centuries. The Mayas made their hot drink from powdered cocoa beans.

Chocolate was so special to the Mayas that the cocoa beans were also used for money. In the Mayan society, a slave was worth one hundred cocoa beans. Because cocoa beans were so valuable, counterfeiters sometimes filled empty bean shells with dirt or sand and passed them off as real beans. If caught, the counterfeiter was made a slave. Poor people could rarely afford the extravagance of grinding up their money to make a hot drink.

Cocoa beans growing on the tree (above) and being harvested (left)

Mayan Eras

As early as 6000 B.C., groups of people in the Valley of Mexico and lands east had turned from hunting for food to growing squash and other foods. Some were growing cotton. By 3500 B.C., farming villages were planting corn and other crops as well. At this early date, there are mysterious evidences of an amazing civilization called the Olmecs. Six-foot stone sculptures of the heads of kings have been found scattered throughout the jungle. But little else is known about these people.

The earliest traces archaeologists have found of Mayan-speaking villages date from 2500 B.C. These villages contained groups of houses surrounded by fields. Some places had public buildings, possibly for religious and government reasons.

For twenty-five centuries the Mayas made farms and homes in the jungles, rain forests, and high plateaus. The Mayas prospered; the population increased. Villages grew large, containing many families and extended families. People spent more time building and decorating their houses; they built more and more public buildings. By A.D. 250, these people dominated the region. Instead of villages, they built complex cities.

Olmec head statue

Mayan Lands

Location—125,000 square miles of Mexico and Central America contain much of what we recognize as ancient Mayan land.

Topography—The Yucatán Peninsula is a lowland with thin soil; the central Mayan lands are mainly rain forest; the southernmost land rises into mountains and plateaus.

Natural Resources—The rain forest and highlands of the area offer rich sources of lumber and good places to grow coffee, cotton, rubber trees, spices, and bananas, among many other things. The northern part of the area provides the right conditions for growing cocoa, sugar cane, and other crops. Many minerals, natural lakes, and rivers can be found throughout the region.

Climate—The northern part of the Yucatán Peninsula is dry, receiving only 51 to 102 centimeters (20 to 40 inches) of rain per year. The southern part receives more. The temperatures in the peninsula range from 68°F to over 86°F. Lands farther south have temperatures averaging around 80°F and receive almost daily rain. The mountains in the southernmost region have a mild climate and get 51 to 76 centimeters (20 to 30 inches) of rain per year.

Geography and Culture—The varied climate and topography allowed the people to develop many crops and eventually to establish large cities. The cities became the cultural centers of Mayan society. Today most people in the area are descendants of the Mayas.

ancient Mayan civilization

● ancient cities

Between A.D. 250 and 900, the Mayas made great advances in art, architecture, and literature. For six centuries, the Mayas wrote hundreds of books, made thousands of sculptures, constructed huge palaces and temples, built

Mayan ruins, Uxmal, Mexico (above and below)

irrigation systems for their fields, studied the stars, composed music and songs, and played games. They traded regularly within the network of their own cities and with other peoples.

Today many of the buildings and statues lie in ruins. The roads the traders used can still be seen, and the music is still played by Mayan descendants. Irrigation systems lie unused; ball courts are waiting for players. But almost all the Mayan books are gone, and with them, much information about how the Mayas really lived and thought.

Writing Books

Unlike any other people in the ancient Americas, the Mayas had a way of writing *sounds,* not just making pictures of objects or ideas. Thus, anything that could be spoken could also be written. Why is this ability significant? There is no limit to the amount or kind of information that can be recorded.

Furthermore, the Mayas made books of their writings. They wrote on long strips of bark from wild fig trees. To make this "paper," the Mayas pulled bark off the fig trees and soaked it in water to remove the sap, and then they beat the strips with ridged wooden hammers. In two or three days, the fibers in the bark stretched out, making a wide, flat surface. This material was then cut into strips about eight inches wide and up to several yards long.

The strips were coated for strength with a thin layer of a gummy substance and then painted over with lime to make a white surface. Scribes then wrote and drew on the paper with paints made from vegetables and minerals. When the strips were dry, they were folded in an accordion fashion and bound between wooden covers.

Today only three Mayan books are known to exist. One is almost complete; it contains observations about the planet Venus and charts used to predict solar eclipses. But it does not tell anything about Mayan customs or history. Nor does it give any clues to the biggest Mayan mystery of all.

Mayan temple, Edzná, Mexico

Around A.D. 900, the Mayas seem to have fled their cities. There are no carvings with dates after A.D. 889. No one knows what happened. Many places seem to have been left in a hurry. And the belongings left behind suggest that the people meant to return. But they never did—at least not to rebuild. For six hundred years, they lived in other cities and places, never regaining their former power.

Some archaeologists believe that a famine drove the people away. Others think that war may have ended the great civilization. Still others think that the way of life in Mayan cities—full of rituals and religious superstitions—may have caused the people to rebel. Perhaps a combination of all these reasons brought the society down.

The Mayan civilization continued in fragmented form in smaller towns and in cultures of other peoples. But then Spanish explorers arrived in 1520. Once the explorers found a few gold figures in the Mayan ruins, they believed that much more was to be had. From then on, the Spanish determined to overcome the Mayas with force and with religion—often with both.

One priest, named Diego de Landa, used every means to make the Mayas accept Roman Catholicism. He had those who refused his religion stretched on pulleys and burned with candles. He had an entire library of Mayan books burned on July 12, 1562, because they contained only "superstition

and lies of the devil." In an effort to communicate with the Mayan people, Landa became a careful student of their ways and tried to translate their symbolic writing into Spanish. Landa's writings give us much of the information we have today about the Mayas of the 1500s and their ancient ancestors. The rest of the information must be painstakingly gathered from the stones and artifacts in Mayan lands.

Mayan stele (left) and carvings (below), Copán, Honduras

Mayan People

According to Landa, the Mayan people were about five feet tall, the women being around four feet, ten inches tall and the men just slightly over five feet. They all had thick, dark hair. The men wore their long hair in braids around the crowns of their heads with one braid down the back. Women wore several hairstyles, most using braids with ribbons coiled around their heads.

The Mayas seem to have preferred long noses and sloping foreheads. They would improve their looks with clay, creating a ridge from the top of the forehead to the bridge of the nose. The true sign of beauty, the sloping head, had to be formed early in life. Parents bound newborns' heads between boards until the soft bones grew into a slanted, almost cone shape.

Mayas also thought crossed eyes were best, perhaps because one of their gods was cross-eyed. To achieve this look, parents hung a bead between the babies' eyes; after the babies looked at the beads for months, their eyes grew permanently crossed.

When older, the Mayas added other features to their appearances. Most young men shaved their foreheads to show off their slanting brows. They also tattooed symbols on their arms, legs, and faces. Many had their ears pierced—but not as people do today. The men wore earplugs in holes sliced into their lobes. They kept adding bigger and bigger plugs until the holes were the size of golf balls. Into these ear holes they placed disks of jade or shell.

Both men and women would often file their teeth to points and inlay them with jade. How do you think modern people know how these ancient Mayas looked? We can tell from sculptures and paintings that the Mayas made.

Mayas took frequent baths, a practice shunned and feared in Europe at the time. They liked perfume that they made from flowers and herbs. Most of the men carried mirrors to check their appearance from time to time.

This mural by Diego Rivera helps us see how the ancient Mayas may have looked and dressed.

The Mayan society had several levels. At the top was the ruler, the absolute king. He was called, in at least some Mayan cities, *makina,* the "great sun lord," and *halach uinic,* the "true man." Like the Egyptians, the Mayas believed that the kings were descended from the gods and that they should be obeyed without question. The kings, in return, would speak to the gods on behalf of the people.

Just below the kings in power were the priests. There were at least four classes of priests. The highest ranking priests were in charge of all the others. They taught writing, astronomy, mathematics, and all rituals associated with the Mayan religion.

Lower ranks included priests who treated sickness. Sometimes the cure was more dangerous than the illness. Nosebleeds, for example, required a priest to cut the foot of the sufferer to let him bleed freely. Other priests were fortune-tellers. They probably ate leaves and mushrooms that caused them to have hallucinations. And another group of priests had the duty of cutting the hearts from the people sacrificed to the gods.

Also high ranking were the nobles. It was from this class that all the priests came. The nobles, men and women, were educated, and they held important positions in the government. The man in charge of the armies, the *batab,* was a member of this class.

Lesser nobles included the artists and architects, traders and scribes, advisors and engineers. Although they did not have the high positions of the first class of nobles, they had many of the privileges. No nobleman or noblewoman had to do common work, such as grinding corn, planting crops, or cleaning. Such labors were left to the common people.

The peasants did the hard manual work of the Mayan society. They grew, harvested, and processed the food. They grew the cotton and produced the fabrics. They tended the buildings. They were the soldiers for the armies and the laborers for construction of the monuments and temples. They were the ordinary people who made the extraordinary visions of the architects, artists, and kings a reality.

At the bottom of society was the slave. Anyone who was in debt or who had committed a crime was considered a slave, the property of another. Sometimes prisoners of war were kept as slaves as well. Important prisoners were used for sacrifices; lesser ones were made to work.

Most Mayas wore simple cotton clothes. The men wore tunics and breech-cloths, sometimes with a short cape. The women wore straight, plain dresses or wraparound skirts and long blouses. Both men and women wore a lot of jewelry: earrings, rings, armbands, and necklaces, all made of shells, volcanic rock, animal teeth and bones, or jade. They either went barefoot or wore sandals of straw and rope.

The Mayas obtained feathers of many brilliant colors from native birds.

Rich people wore the same things, only with more embellishments, such as feathers woven into the fabric. Their shoes were made of deerskin. The kings wore jaguar skins and jade breastplates. The three-foot plumes in their headdresses and on their clothes came from the quetzal, a beautiful bird of the rain forests. The kings had jade bands on their wrists and ankles and gold rings on their toes. To the common Maya, a king's appearance must have been dazzling indeed.

A modern Mayan home

Mayan Life

The classes of Mayan society were reflected in places people lived. The kings lived in palaces, huge monuments covering many acres. Nobles lived in large houses near the center of the city—the closer to the center, the more impressive. The houses had stucco walls and many airy rooms. Rooms may have been divided with embroidered cotton draperies. Some houses even had plumbing and, possibly, fireplaces or ovens.

While the kings, priests, and nobility practiced their ceremonies, waged wars on neighbors, and planned huge building projects, the average Maya led a far quieter and simpler life. Most peasant families lived in small wooden houses with grass-thatched roofs.

Before four o'clock in the morning, women were awake and building fires. By five o'clock the men and boys had eaten breakfast—usually a warmed-up *tortilla*—and were tending to the crops. When planting corn in swampy places or on riverbanks, farmers made ridges in the soil and poked holes into the ridges with a planting stick. Another person came behind, dropping in corn kernels and covering the holes.

In the dry seasons, farmers went into the rain forests and cut down trees. They burned the stumps and the underbrush. In the ashes they planted corn. The corn grew well for a year or two, but such soil wore out quickly. The only remedy was to move to a new place to cut and burn again. Farmers gave part of all they grew to the upper classes of people.

The women worked all day grinding grain in stone bowls or making thread from cotton for the looms. They wove cloth and made clothes, kept the houses, and tended the children. Even the little girls helped make tortillas and other food. The big meal of the day, which usually included beans, fruits, *tamales,* and, occasionally, meat, came in the late afternoon. A favorite drink, *pozole,* was made from corn paste and water, sometimes mixed with honey. Women and girls made the meal, served it to the men and boys, and ate later.

There were days when no one had to work, however, and favorite foods, like chocolate, abounded. Special celebrations were attended by everyone. The most popular event seems to have been a ball game called *pok-to-pok.* Every Mayan city had a ball court—one city had seven courts. Shaped like a capital I, a court measured 100- to 150-feet long and 25- to 50-feet wide. Players, allowed to use only their padded wrists, elbows, and hips, tried to hit a small rubber ball through a vertical hoop or onto a marker on the side of the wall.

Statue of a pok-to-pok player (above) and a ball court at Chichén Itza, Mexico (left)

Only the nobles could play pok-to-pok, but everyone in the city watched. Many nobles placed bets on the outcome, losing much property or many slaves when their wagers were wrong.

All such events took place in the plazas of the cities. Some cities had courts and markets made especially for buying, selling, celebrating, and playing games. The city centers were busy places when people came to trade vegetables, animals, jewelry, jade, pottery, honey, fabrics, and, of course, cocoa beans.

The plazas also saw slave trading. Mayas bought and sold people frequently. Some of the slaves were Mayas. Since Mayan cities had no jails, people who fell behind on their debts, stole, or committed other crimes were made slaves. So were orphans and the children of slaves. Other slaves were stolen, bought, or won in war from neighboring cities.

Ball court temple at Chichén Itzá, Mexico

Mayan Religion

The whole Mayan society, even the popular ball game, was dominated by Mayan religion. Before and after the game, players had to make sacrifices to the gods. Some scholars believe that the players, perhaps the winners, were sacrificed. Everything the Mayas did, from cooking beans to attending ceremonies involving a solar eclipse, had to be done according to ritual. A man about to kill a deer had first to ask the deer to forgive him by saying, "I have need."

Everything, even pottery, was believed to have a spirit. Mayas talked to the objects around them and were always in fear of evil dwarfs who caused sickness and bad crops. To appease the dwarfs, Mayas put out food for them. If illness or bad crops came, a priest prescribed medicine or performed a ritual. Some of the medicines, made from herbs and other plants, were good and often cured the illnesses. Other "cures," however, were far worse than the disease.

The Mayas thought that the world was a flat square that was atop a giant crocodile god in a lily pond. When a person died, he was expected to leave the square and go to one of nine underworlds or thirteen heavens, each under the control of a separate god.

Mayas believed that almost everything had its own god: the sea, the moon, bees, medicine, corn, the sun, life, death, days of the calendar, and so on. Since there were so many gods and so many rules about how to please each god, the Mayas had to depend on the priests to keep everything in order.

Of all the rituals of the Mayan religion, the one most often written about is the human sacrifice. Like other ancient religions, such as that practiced by the priests of Baal, the Mayan religion taught that the gods must be satisfied with human blood. Sometimes the king and his wife would cut themselves and catch the blood on special paper. But on rarer occasions, when the king was gravely ill or the country had experienced a long famine, priests took slaves to the temple altars and killed them and put the blood on the statues of the gods.

Mayan corn god (left) and sacrificial altar (above)

For all their care to obey the priests and please the gods, the Mayas feared death greatly. Only priests, warriors who had died in battle, people who had hanged themselves, and people who had been sacrificed by the priests could be sure of getting into Mayan paradise. All others, no matter how well they had kept the rules, might—by the whim of some god—be condemned to the underworld.

When someone died, he was mourned for days. He was buried according to his station in life. The common people were often buried under their houses, which were then abandoned by the others who lived there. The rich could afford tombs with heavy stone coverings, elaborately engraved.

Almost everyone, regardless of his class, had a piece of jade in his mouth so that he would have some money in the next life.

Kings were buried with great ceremony and wealth. One king, Pacal, was buried in a large room under a Mayan pyramid. Buried with him were six other people and a huge cache of jade jewelry and other treasures. This king had a jade mask over his face, perhaps to show his power in the afterlife.

This relief carving, possibly depicting Pacal, is on a wall in Palenque, Mexico (Pacal's city).

Modern descendants of the Mayas

Mayas Today

In 1960 a man exploring a cave came upon a series of rooms holding many Mayan artifacts and paintings. When he told about his find, a Mayan priest from a nearby village came and demanded that he be allowed to perform ceremonies to pacify the gods of rain whose cave had been violated. It had probably been a thousand years since anyone had been inside that cave. But after all that time, the Mayan way still held power over the Mayan descendants.

As many as two million descendants of the Mayas are living in the region today. A few still weave cloth, plant and harvest corn, and practice some rituals as the ancient Mayas did. Some still use the same calendars and speak languages quite close to what Pacal and his people may have spoken, although neither would probably be able to understand the other.

Mayan life is now a mix of Mayan, Roman Catholic, and modern ideas. Some farmers plant their fields with the same prayers that were said in ancient times. But in other places, the great-great-great-great-great-grandchildren of the Mayas are reading about their ancestors on their computers. What might an ancient Maya think of the hot chocolate those grandchildren are drinking, made from a packet of powder that even commoners can obtain?

To Think Like an Archaeologist

1. Get Notebook pages 52 and 53, the papers your teacher gives you, a pen or pencil, and a stapler.

2. Form an archaeological team with your Heritage Studies partner. Make observations about the "finds" reported in the papers you have received from your teacher.

3. Produce a booklet based on your conclusions. Share your observations and opinions with other teams.

9

Story Keepers and Kings:
Ancient Africa

Voices called from the rain forest—not human voices, but voices of birds and monkeys and insects. The sun blazed down on Namasha, warming her bare arms, and turned the distant river to gold. She glanced around her at the faces of the other village children. Their eyes were fixed on the storyteller.

"This is a tale of how the mountains came to be," said the old man seated before them. "Long, long ago, before any of us were born, the earth was smooth and flat like this river stone I hold in my hand. But one day, the earth decided to have a conversation with the sky. She rose up high, higher than birds fly, until she touched the sky. The earth and the sky told one another their secrets. When they finished talking, the earth bade the sky good-bye and started to return to her place. But on the way down, she became very tired. Parts of her became so tired that they stopped right where they were, before reaching the ground. Now we call these parts mountains and hills."

Namasha swatted at a fly and yawned. She liked the old man's stories, but she had heard this one before. She had heard most of his stories before. Stories about mountains and rivers and lakes and animals. Stories about the ancient people who had lived here before.

Namasha squinted beyond the old man toward the river. She remembered the old Congolese proverb her father often quoted: "No matter how full the river, it still wants to grow." She wanted to grow. She wanted to hear new stories. When would the storyteller give them something new?

The Dark Continent

For hundreds of years Europeans called Africa "the Dark Continent" because they knew almost nothing about Africa or its many people. After explorers visited Africa and told of their findings, however, the European world learned a great deal about the continent. They learned that Africa has large lakes, grand mountain ranges, mighty rivers, vast deserts, and lush rain forests.

Sand dunes, Sahara Desert

Africa is both a dry and a wet land. If you were to walk along the equator, you would be walking right through the heart of Africa. It is the only continent to have deserts both north and south of the equator. The Sahara, the largest desert in the world, almost completely covers the northern half of Africa. The Kalahari and Namib Deserts are in southern Africa. To the east, by the *Horn of Africa* where Somalia is today, lies another desert area. Somalia receives little rain because winds blow most of the water vapor into the mountains of Ethiopia before it reaches Somalia. What would you call an area like this? Somalia is called a *rain shadow*.

Africa is also home to many lakes and rivers. Lake Victoria, in East Africa, is the source of the Nile River, the longest river in the world. Lake Chad supplies water for four different African countries. Lakes Nasser and Volta, both manmade lakes, supply electricity.

Study the map of Africa on the next page. How many different rivers can you find?

Waterfall, Cameroon

Africa

Location—A large continent to the southwest of Asia; includes the islands of Madagascar, Comoros, Réunion, Mauritius, Canary, and Seychelles in the Indian Ocean. Africa is divided almost in half by the equator.

Climate—Much of the climate is tropical, with warm temperatures during the day and cool temperatures at night; other parts have a dry desert climate. Temperatures in the Sahara range from 50°F in the winter to 100°F in the summer. In northern Somalia, summer temperatures of 115°F or more are common.

Topography—Deserts cover about two-fifths of Africa's land. Africa also has mountain ranges, rivers, rain forests, beautiful lakes, and savannas.

Natural Resources—Rich in mineral resources, Africa has gold, petroleum, oil, copper, diamonds, and natural gas.

Geography and Culture—For many centuries, the Sahara kept Africa isolated from European culture because Europeans traded only along the coast, never venturing inland.

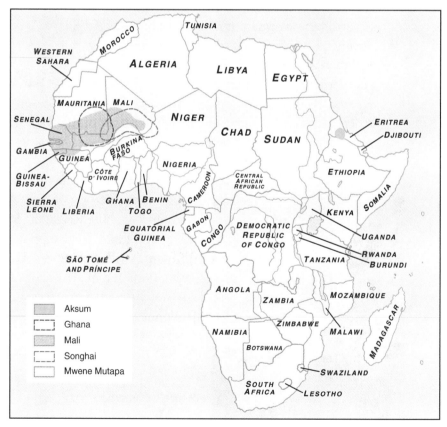

Everything in Africa seems bigger than life. Consider its mountains, for example. Mount Kilimanjaro, in Tanzania, is over nineteen thousand feet high. This mountain and others, such as those in the Sahara Desert, were formed by volcanic activity. Many volcanic mountains are over twelve thousand feet high. Africa also contains mountains formed by earthquakes.

Africa has the largest tropical area of any continent. Much of the Tropics is made up of rain forests. Some areas just north and south of the equator receive as much as eighty inches of rainfall per year. Rain forests are filled with huge trees and vines, but their soil is not very fertile. The constant rain washes many nutrients out of the soil, making it difficult for farmers to raise good crops there.

The area between the Sahara and Kalahari Deserts, excluding the rain forest, is called the *savanna*. With tall grasses and widely spaced trees, the savanna is a good place to raise crops and cattle. Wild animals live on the savanna too. Antelope, giraffes, zebras, elephants, leopards, and lions are just a few of the animals that roam this grassy space.

Mount Kilimanjaro

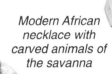

Modern African necklace with carved animals of the savanna

Zebras on the savanna

195

Keys to Africa's Past

We often learn about people and their history from what we read in books. We know that the Egyptians left written records on both stone and papyri. But most of the people of Africa did not have a written language. How then can we know anything about them? There are many ways of learning about people other than by reading written records.

Linguistics

One way is to study the spread of languages. Long ago the *Bantu,* an early African people, left their homes on the Benue River and traveled into central and eventually eastern and southern Africa. Moving to another region is called *migrating.* When the Bantu migrated, they took their language with them. After settling in a new area, they had to learn to speak with the people already living there. Both groups shared and borrowed bits of language—a word or two, or a new way of saying something. Slowly, each language changed.

Linguists, people who study languages and the ways they change, can discover where people went by the words and grammar that they lent and borrowed. Linguists helped trace the migration route of the Bantu.

Botany

Linguists follow people through changes in their language. *Botanists,* who study plants, trace the movements of people by their crops. When the Bantu farmers moved to new homes, they took seeds with them so that they could plant crops to feed their families. The whole Bantu migration took about fifteen hundred years and covered half of the continent of Africa.

By tracking the spread of their crops, botanists helped trace the migration routes of the Bantu.

African crops

Archaeology

Ancient African rock painting

Another important source of information comes from archaeology. In some areas of Africa, archaeologists have found caves with paintings on the walls. From these drawings we know about the weapons that the early African people used for fighting and hunting, as well as what animals they hunted. Some of the paintings are accompanied by symbols that may have been part of a written language. Unfortunately, no one has discovered what these symbols mean.

Oral History

Do you have an older friend or relative who tells stories about the times when he or she was a child? Such stories are called oral history because they are spoken and not written.

Most African villages, like Namasha's, had at least one person who was the official rememberer. It was his job to learn the village's history. He taught the children and reminded the adults of their past. He described the journeys of their ancestors when they looked for new farmland. He told of the deeds of past leaders and heroes. And he reminded the villagers of their ancient traditions.

The village rememberer told his stories at every opportunity. He wanted to keep the village's history from being forgotten. Modern historians know that oral history is important in learning about the past of Africa.

In Africa, jewelry can sometimes tell a person's tribe, age, marital or financial status, social standing, or accomplishments.

To Preserve History Orally

1. Think of an important event in the history of your family, such as an adventurous experience or a meaningful accomplishment. It should be something you could tell about in less than three minutes.

2. In your group, tell your own story and listen to the stories of the other group members, trying to remember the details of each story.

3. Now find a student from another group. Tell him your own story and the stories of your group members. Listen as he tells you his story and the other stories from his group. Do you think you could remember all of these stories to tell to someone else?

Africa's People

Africa was home to many different people. In the north lived the nomads of the Sahara. The greatest of these nomadic people were the *Tuareg*.

Imagine seeing a group of warriors, dressed in loose, flowing garments and riding swift camels, coming toward you in a cloud of sand. As one of the men comes closer, you see that his head is wrapped with a long piece of dark blue cotton that acts as both a turban and a veil. His face is hidden except for a narrow slit for his eyes. The Tuareg frequently attacked caravans in bands. They even attacked towns built on the edges of the desert.

The camel helped the Tuareg become the most feared of the desert peoples. Camels had been introduced into northern Africa shortly after the birth of Christ. Though ill-tempered and stubborn, the camel was a necessity because of its ability to survive and work in the desert. With camels, the Tuareg could move freely across the Sahara. They also used camel hides to make their tents, and from camel milk they made butter and cheese.

In the grassy savanna and the forests southwest of the Sahara lived many prosperous people. Some farmed the fertile soil. Others built cities and sent their goods across the Sahara to the Mediterranean coast. These peoples formed great empires to protect themselves and their trade routes.

The Nilotic people originally lived in the area of the modern country of Sudan. Then they migrated to the shores of Lake Victoria and into the modern countries of Kenya, Tanzania, and Uganda. Perhaps the best known of these peoples are the tall and slender Masai. They measured their wealth and social standing by the number of cattle they owned.

Much of the rest of Africa was settled by the Bantu, who migrated from the Benue River. They wandered south and settled in the Congo Basin. For perhaps two hundred years or more, the Bantu prospered and their numbers grew. Finally, the land could support no more villages, and some of the Bantu packed their belongings and moved southeast once more, all the way to the tip of Africa.

A modern Masai tribesman

A Bantu carved figure

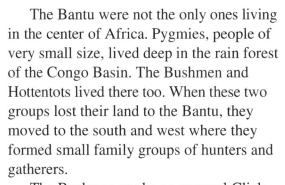

The Bantu were not the only ones living in the center of Africa. Pygmies, people of very small size, lived deep in the rain forest of the Congo Basin. The Bushmen and Hottentots lived there too. When these two groups lost their land to the Bantu, they moved to the south and west where they formed small family groups of hunters and gatherers.

The Bushmen spoke an unusual Click language. Think of all the noises you can make with your tongue, teeth, and lips that are not words at all. In a Click language, these sounds have meaning. Try talking to a friend and adding a few clicks and pops as you speak. It is not easy!

Europeans also lived in Africa. In the middle of the seventeenth century, the Dutch set up a station to provide water and food for ships on their way to India. The Dutch found a beautiful place on the southern tip of Africa and decided it would be a good place to live. Englishmen joined them about one hundred fifty years later. Both the Dutch and the English have lived there ever since.

A pygmy man

African Empires

Aksum

Stele of Aksum

On the east side of Africa lies the modern nation of Ethiopia. Long before the birth of Christ, farmers settled in this area and eventually built the empire of Aksum. Aksum was a wealthy and powerful kingdom. It supplied precious stones, incense, gold, ivory, ebony, myrrh, and elephants to the Egyptian pharaohs. Archaeologists who have studied the ruins of Aksum tell us that walled castles dominated the capital city. Aksum's educated people spoke Greek. Linguists believe that the Aksumites visited the Greek city of Byzantium often, perhaps to trade.

King Ezana ruled the empire of Aksum. He wore gold jewelry and rich clothing, and he rode in a golden chariot drawn by four elephants. Under King Ezana, Aksum became the strongest country in East Africa, conquering neighboring kingdoms.

After Ezana conquered the people of Kush, he is recorded as giving thanks to the Lord for the victory. Ezana had become a Christian. Christianity was probably introduced into Aksum by Byzantine traders during the reign of Constantine. With Ezana's conversion, Christianity became Aksum's state religion.

After the fall of Rome, Aksum's trade dwindled. Then in the seventh century, Muslim armies conquered Egypt and cut Aksum off from its trade with the Mediterranean world. The power of the kings declined as the kingdom grew poorer. When the nobility rebelled and divided Aksum among themselves, the kingdom disappeared.

In the grassy savanna, Africans founded three great empires: Ghana, Mali, and Songhai. You can see the outlines of these empires on the map on page 194.

Ghana

No one knows who founded Ghana, but the kingdom probably appeared about three hundred years after the birth of Christ. By the eighth century A.D., Ghana was an empire. Ghana was governed by African kings, but many Arab merchants also lived in Ghana. Much of what we know about this empire comes from their accounts.

Gold mines were found on the land adjoining the king- dom of Ghana. Ghana did not own the gold mines, but their mer- chants traded for the gold in a unique way. The traders never saw

The ancient empire of Ghana was once located in present-day Mauritania.

one another. Great peoples of the Sudan, who lived on the land with the mines, set up a boundary that no one could cross. The merchants from Ghana would place wares and cloth on the boundary line and leave. Then the people of the Sudan would bring gold and leave it beside the merchandise before retreating. The merchants would then return to take the gold. If they were not satisfied with the amount of gold the Sudan people had left, they would go away again and wait for the people to add more gold until the price for the merchandise was acceptable.

The merchants of Ghana traded the gold—along with cola nuts, honey, and slaves—for copper, dried fruit, cowrie shells, and salt from the salt mines of the Sahara. They also traded for horses, cloth, swords, and books from North Africa and Europe.

Ghana had so much gold that the king was afraid its value would go down, so he decreed that the gold would always have a certain value. The king also taxed all trade. He was fabulously rich.

Ghana consisted of two towns. One town was Muslim. The other town, where the king lived, practiced a religion that involved sorcery. Between the two towns were all the houses of the kingdom's people.

Many African towns are still Muslim, with people worshiping in mosques such as the one above.

Ghana's army and cavalry protected its trade. When the Arabs heard of the wealth of Ghana, their leader sent his army across the Sahara to attack Ghana's capital city. After a ten-year siege, the Arabs conquered and destroyed the city. These wars interrupted trade and weakened Ghana's kings. When the army of Mali attacked, the empire could not fight back. The empire of Ghana ended in 1203.

Mali

The empire of Mali included all of Ghana and much more land besides. No one knows who founded Mali, but by 1225 its ruler, Sundiata, had conquered Ghana. In just a few years, Sundiata gained control of the gold and salt trade and built his capital on the main trade route across the Sahara.

Ibn Battuta, a traveler from Tangier, visited Mali from 1352 to 1353. He described the people of Mali as lovers of justice and honesty. Travelers in the kingdom felt completely free from fear of harm by robbers. Although the people of Mali did many good deeds, they did not follow Christ. The Islamic religion dominated the kingdom.

This great empire was weakened by quarrels over who would become the next ruler. The fighting inside the empire encouraged enemies on the outside to attack. After four hundred years, Mali was once again a small village on the banks of the Niger River.

Muslim school in modern Mali

Mansa Musa

The most famous of all the Mali emperors was Mansa Musa. Mansa was his title; Musa, his name. He ruled from 1312 to 1337. He became famous, not because he was a brave general or a wise lawgiver but because he was rich.

Mansa Musa was a Muslim. In 1324 he made a pilgrimage to Mecca. At the front of his caravan marched five hundred slaves, each carrying a six-pound staff of gold. One hundred camels followed behind Mansa Musa, each carrying three hundred pounds of gold. If the value of an ounce of gold is $375, the total value of Musa's gold was about $200 million.

Mansa Musa wore gold jewelry and dressed extravagantly in velvet tunics. He had a large silk tent in the palace yard, where he met with members of his court. Slaves and musicians surrounded him during public appearances, making a great ceremony of everything he did.

In spite of his love of pomp and extravagance, Mansa Musa was very generous. He gave money freely to officials, shopkeepers, and charities everywhere he went.

Songhai

Songhai had been an important town in the empire of Mali. Like Mali, it depended on trade and sent merchants to Spain, Tunis, and Egypt. In the fifteenth century under the leadership of Sunni Ali, Songhai won its independence.

Sunni Ali was a man of war, and he was never defeated. Some people believed that he was a magician who could change himself, his horses, and his soldiers into other creatures or even make them invisible. Sunni Ali fought Mali for twenty-eight years. Eventually he controlled all of the trade routes and the best farm-land. Sunni Ali built a fleet of canoes to patrol the Niger River. He also built several capital cities to rule his empire better.

Timbuktu

The ancient city of Timbuktu became Songhai's center of Islamic faith and learning. It looked as though no one would ever be able to defeat the empire of Songhai.

Finally Morocco, one of Songhai's neighbors to the north, attacked Songhai. The Moroccan army had muskets, and its soldiers were better disciplined than Songhai's. The army of Songhai was defeated, and its government was destroyed.

Now other enemies attacked Songhai over and over again. Famine struck and then plague. Soon the empire of Songhai disappeared. In its place appeared many smaller states that constantly fought each other over land and trade.

Mwene Mutapa

Far to the south of Ghana, Mali, and Songhai in the modern country of Zimbabwe lie many ruins of stone walls and buildings—the ruins of the kingdom Mwene Mutapa. Archaeologists believe these ruins date from the eighth century.

The first settlers in ancient Zimbabwe were ancestors of the Shona, or Mashona, as they were called. They moved across the Zambezi River to have more room to live and plant crops. They organized themselves into clans and built *zimbabwes,* or big stone houses.

One zimbabwe is a huge fortress with intricate passageways and numerous rooms. It may have been the king's house. In the valley nearby is a stone ruin that may have been a temple. All of these buildings were built of stone without any mortar.

The Shona worshiped their kings as gods. Anyone who wanted to talk with the king had to come into his presence creeping and clapping his hands. Because the king was taught to be a god, he had to be perfect. If he fell ill or was deformed in any way, he was expected to commit suicide.

The Shona were farmers, but they also raised cattle. They found gold along the rivers and streams and traded it for textiles, glass beads, and Chinese porcelain. When the empire grew too big for the land to support, the Shona abandoned their zimbabwes. Archaeologists believe the Shona moved away during the fifteenth century.

The Wall (left) and Shona Village (above), parts of the Zimbabwe National Monument

The Coastal Cities of East Africa

The Shona traded their gold on the east coast of Africa in cities built especially for trade. No one knows who founded these cities. But by the fourth century they were governed by the Omani, Arab kings who lived far away in Oman. Mogadishu was the northernmost city, and Sofala was the southernmost city.

All along the coast, the weather was warm and the waters were full of fish. Farmers raised sheep and grew rice, millet, sorghum, cucumbers, coconuts, sugar cane, oranges, lemons, pomegranates, and bananas.

Omani merchants traded at these cities for ivory and tortoise shells. As the cities grew, more items became available for trade. By the tenth century the Africans were trading timber, gold, iron, amber, saffron, and leopard skins. To Chinese merchants they sent slaves, rhinoceros horns, pearls, incense, myrrh, and *ambergris,* a waxy substance obtained from whales and used in perfumes. One fifteenth-century Chinese emperor even traded with the Africans for a giraffe, which he thought was a unicorn. If you had been able to trade with these coastal cities, what items would you have wanted?

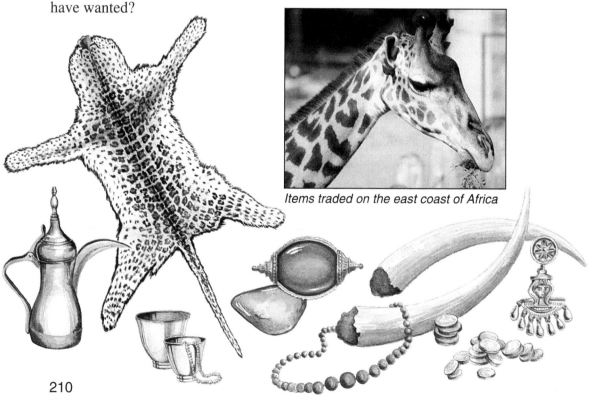

Items traded on the east coast of Africa

Central Africa

The peoples of central Africa had no written language. And few artifacts remain because of the hot, wet climate. We do not know much about the ancient history of these peoples, but we know that they later formed important trading empires. The Nyamwezi controlled the trade routes to the east coast of Africa for hundreds of years. Their *porters,* or men who carried goods to market, were the best in central Africa.

The culture and customs of Africa had remained unchanged for centuries. But as trade and exploration increased, the Western world gained greater interest in this land they called "the Dark Continent." More and more Europeans came to Africa to trade for slaves and to explore. And some came to preach the gospel.

Missionary David Livingstone, right, and meeting Stanley, below

"And this gospel of the kingdom shall be preached in all the world for a witness unto all nations; and then shall the end come."

Matthew 24:14

Namasha watched the face of this new storyteller. His eyes were kind. His stories did not come from his head—they came from the thick book with the black cover that he carried everywhere.

"In the beginning, God created the world—the sky, the trees, the mountains, the hills, the rivers. And then He created man and woman. He walked on the earth and talked with them and loved them. But then they disobeyed Him. He still loved them, even after they had sinned, so He gave them a gift—His only Son. Jesus Christ came to earth to walk and talk with men and women. He came to die for them because He loved them just as His Father did."

Ever since this new storyteller had come to the village, something had changed. Monkeys and parrots still called from the forest. Light still slanted through the bamboo trees and made crisscrossed shadows on the village paths. The river still rippled in the distance. But something was different.

These stories were new. They were not like the old man's stories that Namasha knew so well. Namasha leaned closer as the missionary held up a picture of a man, torn and bleeding, hanging on a wooden cross. Her throat felt tight. She wanted to hear more of these new stories about Jesus.

Golden Age of the Orient:
Japan, China, India

What do you think of when you hear the word *golden?* Do you think of rich kings and glittering palaces? Or do you think of shiny coins in a treasure chest? We use the word *golden* to refer to such things, but it can also be used to describe a time when a country is at its best. We say that a country at its peak is in its *golden age.*

Listen closely. In the distance you can hear the gongs vibrate in a mysterious melody. Inside, scholars are bent over tables, brushing fine strokes onto paper in a delicate writing of symbols and lines. Outside, in a small building, people in robes and sashes are kneeling before a stone statue. Farther out—out in the fields—are rows and rows of tea plants. You are visiting the Orient.

The Orient refers to countries in the Far East, such as China, Japan, and India. Each of these countries enjoyed a golden age when its culture, art, and literature flourished. These golden periods in the Orient produced many inventions, works of art, and intriguing stories. As you make this journey into the golden age of the Orient, you will meet a people who, though they lived thousands of years ago, made contributions to the modern world.

China's Golden Years

Do you remember what a dynasty is? A *dynasty* is a line of kings and rulers who belong to the same family. In A.D. 618, the Tang rulers came to power in China. For nearly three hundred years, they ruled China. The Song dynasty replaced the Tang dynasty and ruled for about three hundred years. The six hundred years of these two dynasties make up what is called China's golden age (A.D. 618-1279).

During both of these dynasties, trade was an important part of China's economy. The Han dynasty began trade with other countries by opening the Silk Road. The Silk Road was the trade route between China and countries to the west, such as ancient Persia. Through this route, the Chinese traded their famous silk, spices, and fine pottery. How do you think China's trading with other countries affected its culture? The Chinese not only traded their goods with other countries but also shared their ideas and inventions. The golden age in China produced some great pieces of literature and art as well as some important inventions.

A Tang dynasty tomb figure

The Written Word

Writers of the Tang and Song dynasties produced some of China's finest literature. All scholars had to be good writers of both poetry and prose. The test for becoming a government worker required skill in both

Some of nearly fifteen thousand stone tablets at Yunju Temple on which Buddhist monks engraved scriptures for preservation

A Chinese bell and stand

writing styles. Often scholars spent hours in conversation, making up and exchanging poems. Their poems spoke of life, nature, home, friendship, and romance. One collection of forty-eight thousand poems from the Tang dynasty names twenty-two hundred different poets.

China's most famous poets lived during the golden age. Often poets wrote poems to be put to music, especially to the music of common folk tunes. One tune might have several sets of words. Singers performed these songs accompanied by chimes, bells, drums, flutes, and lutes. The scholar did not just write words for music; he also had to be able to play his song on the lute.

A modern Chinese girl playing a pipa

Another type of writing, the writing of history, also became important during the golden age of the Orient. The Tang rulers began a tradition in which each new dynasty wrote the official history of the last dynasty. Historians had to examine piles of court records. Then they decided which events were important and should be included in the history. Scholars who volunteered or were appointed to the task spent several years at this work. Chinese historians prided themselves on keeping accurate, detailed histories. From these records we know much about Chinese life.

Other golden age literature included philosophy, religion, politics, stories, and fables. Writers produced many "how-to" books, giving instruction in painting, handwriting, and gardening. Gardening was important to the Chinese. They created different shapes in their gardens by trimming the bushes to look like miniature mountains and by building small pools to look like lakes and rivers.

All the written works of the Orient, whether in scroll or book form, were kept in government and private libraries. Reading was a favorite pastime for many Chinese people.

An Oriental garden

The Printed Word
Block Printing

One reason that writing and libraries were so common in China was that the Chinese knew how to print books. The Chinese of the Tang dynasty already knew how to make paper. During the golden age, they developed *block printing*.

In block printing, the printer carved a whole page of symbols, or characters, into a block of wood. The characters had to be backwards, much like those on a rubber stamp. Next, he rolled ink onto the raised letters, carefully laid a piece of paper onto the block, and then removed the paper after it was printed. A fast printer could print two thousand pages a day. The oldest known printed book is a block-printed scroll dating from A.D. 868. It is the *Diamond Sutra,* a book sacred to Buddhists.

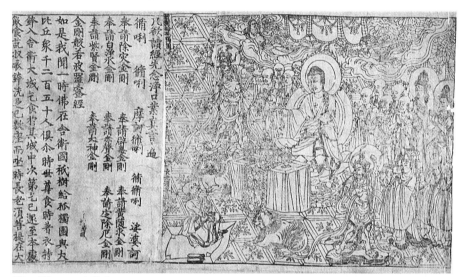

The Diamond Sutra

During the Song dynasty, the Chinese began to use movable-type printing. In movable-type printing, individual characters or letters were carved onto individual wood blocks. The printer then arranged these characters to form a whole page. The blocks could be used again to form a new page. The major problem the Chinese had in using movable type was organizing the more than forty thousand characters of the written Chinese language.

The Chinese printed all types of literature, such as dynastic histories, religious books, almanacs, pamphlets, dictionaries, and prose and poetry collections. Do you remember who Confucius was? He taught the values of having strong character and being responsible. Many of his teachings were printed as a collection of rules and standards of behavior, the Confucian *Classics*.

Movable type, invented by the Chinese of the golden age, was not used in Europe until about four hundred years after it had first been used in China. Today printing is a big part of our lives. Think about the newspapers you read, the words on a cereal box, or even the words on this page. Can you imagine how hard it would be to print everything we need using the Chinese block-printing method?

While we may not print like the early Chinese, our methods still echo their early methods. Computers and electronic devices do much of the work that the ancient printers had to do by hand. What do you think are some of the advantages or disadvantages of the progress we have made in printing methods?

Modern printing

An Age of Invention

Printing was not the only invention of China's golden age. Chinese scholars put their minds to work on several other practical matters. Did you know that gunpowder was first used by the Chinese during the golden age?

The Chinese did not use gunpowder in warfare until the Song dynasty. But earlier, they used it for another purpose. In religious and government celebrations, the Chinese set off firecrackers made with gunpowder. Most Americans associate firecrackers with the Fourth of July, but the Chinese use them to celebrate the New Year. On the first day of the year, every person and animal in China becomes one year older. How would you like to celebrate your birthday this way?

The Chinese New Year falls somewhere in January or February of each year, depending on the moon's position in its yearly cycle. Even today, the Chinese celebrate the New Year with parades, costumes, and firecrackers.

Man, these party favors are really a blast!

The Chinese also discovered the magnetic compass. They found that when a piece of magnetic iron ore was attached to a piece of wood or cork floating in water, it always pointed north-south. The magnetic compass was most useful for guidance on land or navigation at sea.

The Chinese, however, did not use the compass for navigating at first. Instead, they used it for religious and superstitious purposes. The compass aided astrologers in making up the yearly calendar and setting the date of the New Year. Years later, in the Song dynasty, the Chinese began to use the compass for navigation.

Although the early Chinese compasses indicated south rather than north, they operated on the same principle as modern ones.

The Chinese produced other practical devices too. They built highly accurate clocks run by water. They made rain and snow gauges that helped them with flood control. To connect the regions of the empire, they built a system of roads, bridges, and canals. They also made maps. The oldest printed map existing today shows China in 1155.

In medicine, the Chinese studied diseases and recommended treatments. Acupuncture, a medical practice developed during the Han dynasty, continued to be used during the golden age. It is still being used today in some parts of the world.

The Chinese of this period also used various herbs as medicine. In the early twelfth century, the government published the *Imperial Medical Encyclopedia,* a volume listing medical problems with their symptoms and treatments.

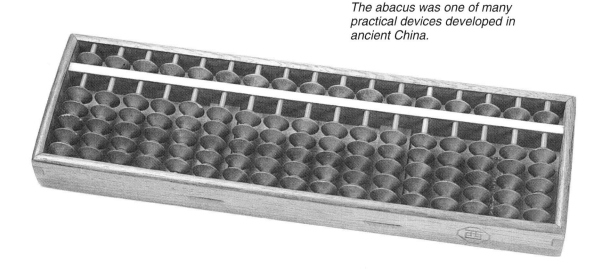

The abacus was one of many practical devices developed in ancient China.

Making Porcelain

The Chinese invented a way of making *porcelain,* a thin, but strong, translucent pottery. Porcelain, or "china," is made from a mixture of white clay and the mineral feldspar. The Chinese tried many combinations to get just the right mixture. The potter worked with this clay mixture, using a potter's wheel or a mold. Once the pottery dried, it was decorated with paint, carvings, or a glaze of liquid glass. Pale green and blue gray were two favorite colors used in porcelain designed by the Chinese in the golden age.

A Song dynasty vase with pale green glaze

After the artist finished his decorating, the pottery was fired in a very hot oven. After the firing, the clay, or porcelain, was hard, shiny, and translucent. Porcelain has a clear, bell-like ring when tapped lightly on the edge. By the end of the Tang period, the Chinese had learned to make beautiful porcelain. Today, old Chinese porcelain is rare and extremely valuable.

The Chinese used porcelain for both practical and decorative purposes. Many families served their daily tea in porcelain cups. The emperor was a major buyer of porcelain goods. He occasionally ordered several thousand pieces of porcelain at a time. Some provinces sent porcelain to the emperor's court as their required *tribute.* A tribute was a payment made to ensure protection or to show submission to the emperor.

An Age of Art

The Chinese distinguished between artists and craftsmen. For example, in making porcelain, only the potter and the decorator were considered artists. The other men who helped were considered craftsmen. The Chinese considered painters to be true artists. Painters usually trained for at least twenty years before they were considered good artists. Like writing poetry, painting became a requirement on the exams that had to be passed before a person could work for the government.

The most common type of painting was landscape painting. A Chinese artist did not paint while he looked at a scene. Instead, he studied the scene for several hours. Then, in his studio, he put down his thoughts of the scene on a silk or paper scroll, using ink and brushes made from animal hairs. Once he had made a stroke, it could not be erased, covered up, or changed. Painters worked quickly, before their thoughts of the view faded.

In China, paintings did not hang on the walls but were on rolled-up scrolls that were stored in cases. The owners of the scrolls displayed the paintings only on special occasions. Visitors and family members enjoyed these works of art that honored nature.

A Chinese calligraphy set

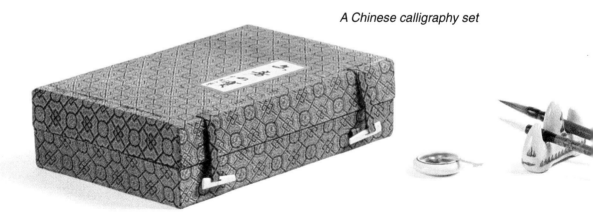

Pagoda temple, Hong Kong

Calligraphy, from the Greek words meaning "beautiful writing," is an art similar to painting. The Chinese did not simply "write" words, but created a series of beautiful symbols. Calligraphers practiced many years, first to learn and then to improve their art. The government even had a special college that taught calligraphy. An excellent calligrapher received great honor and praise in China. Where do you see examples of calligraphy today?

Architecture was also an important art in the golden age. The Chinese believed their buildings should blend into the landscape. They built houses low and long. Wooden pillars and beams supported the roofs of the houses, while the walls were simply screens decorated with carvings, paintings, or lacquer, a clear and shiny coating.

Roofs having curved eaves came into use during the Tang dynasty and soon became typical of Chinese architecture. Another Chinese building style begun during this age was the *pagoda*. Pagodas were first used as Buddhist temples. Soon, however, the pagoda was just another type of building used for many purposes.

Japan's Golden Years

China's Influence

Stone Buddha, Kyoto

Who do you think causes more changes in a country—people who trade with the citizens of the country or people who come to live there? During China's golden age, Buddhist missionaries were sent to neighboring countries. Many of these missionaries went to live in Japan, bringing new styles of clothing, new ideas, new customs, and a new religion.

The Buddhist missionaries had a great influence on Japan. Many Buddhist missionaries were scholars and teachers. Besides teaching the Japanese about Buddhism, these missionaries also taught the Japanese how to read and write Chinese, study Chinese literature, and create art in the Chinese style. Later, many Japanese traveled to China to study in the Buddhist schools. This travel between China and Japan caused Chinese ideas and customs to influence Japan greatly.

Buddhism was not the only religion in Japan, however. Shintoism was, and still is, the main religion of Japan. Shinto means "the way of the gods" and teaches that every object or creature in nature has a god. So, in Shintoism, many gods are worshiped. How is this type of worship different from what the Bible teaches? A big part of Shintoism is emperor worship. The Japanese believed that the emperor descended from the sun goddess's grandson, *Jimmu Tenno,* and so deserved to be worshiped.

A torii marking the entrance to a Shinto shrine in Miyazima

226

Early Japanese society was made of *clans.* A clan is a group of people who claim to have a common ancestor. The many clans of Japan fought among themselves for control of other clans and land. Finally, the *Yamato* clan gained the most power. The leader of the Yamato clan claimed to be related to Jimmu Tenno, the legendary grandson of the sun goddess. This supposed ancestry allowed the leader of the Yamato clan to claim the title of emperor. Chinese culture first entered Japan in the fourth century A.D., during the early centuries of the Yamato rule.

In the seventh century, the Yamato rulers started a new program in Japan. This program was aimed at making Japan much like Tang China by improving the government system. The Japanese admired the achievements of the Chinese and wanted this progress in their own land.

The first Japanese capital was set up in *Nara.* It was the capital of the Yamato rule and also the center of Japanese Buddhism. The Yamato wanted to lessen the power of the Buddhists because that religious movement kept getting stronger. The Yamato moved the capital to a new location, Heian-kyo. This city became the center of culture and the arts, opening the doors to Japan's golden age.

Seventh-century carving, Nara Prefecture

Monuments on a mountain trail, Nara Prefecture

The Heian Age

Soon after the capital was moved to Heian-kyo, another family, the *Fujiwara,* came into power. The Chinese continued to influence Japan under the Fujiwara rule. The Japanese looked to China as a model to follow. However, the Japanese changed the Chinese patterns and made them part of their own Japanese culture. Much of the typical Japanese culture had its start in the court life at Heian.

Chinese learning greatly influenced Japanese learning at Heian. Japanese students learned to read and write Chinese and to memorize Chinese poetry. In Japan, however, only the nobility attended school. Government positions were open only to nobles. The Japanese government did not emphasize education as much as the Chinese government did. Family background, wealth, and social position were more important than ability in holding government positions.

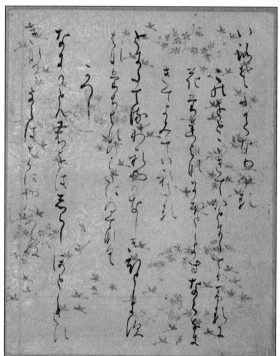

In addition to teaching Chinese culture, Japanese education also included much instruction in court *etiquette,* or manners. Life at the Heian court demanded strict rules of behavior. Every situation had a proper action and response, from accepting a piece of food to meeting the emperor. Above all, a person at the court must have *composure* and not show his emotions at any time. If someone did not follow these rules, he was not welcome at court.

This fragment of Japanese poetry is from the Ise Shu, *an anthology of poems by Lady Ise, composed during the Fujiwara period (early 12th century, ink on decorated paper; collection Osaragi Jiro, Japan).*

The Spoken Word

The Japanese had their own language; however, Chinese was the official language of the court. Japanese scholars spent many years learning Chinese. Often, how far a man was promoted at court depended upon how well he spoke Chinese. For centuries, all the official writing in the Japanese court was done in Chinese. Histories, diaries, and poetry were all written in Chinese by nobles at court.

Although the Japanese had a spoken language, they had no written language. Japanese differed greatly from Chinese, but the Japanese adopted Chinese characters and made them fit their own language. This process took place over many years during the Heian period. Even today, Japanese is a difficult language to master.

家

Japanese character for "house"

The Written Word

Japan's Golden Age of Literature

The Japanese language became common during the Heian period; it was used for unofficial writing. In fact, the Heian period is known as the golden age of literature in Japan. Japanese literature was written mainly by ladies who were wealthy. They wrote in Japanese because women were not thought capable of learning Chinese; therefore, they were never taught the Chinese language. These women often spent their leisure time writing about their experiences in the emperor's court.

These writings provide a complete picture of life for the wealthy. One Heian woman wrote the first Japanese novel. Her six-volume *Tale of Genji* tells the story of Prince Genji and his life at court.

Poetry was an important part of Japanese culture. A person was judged by how well he could create a poem. One special type of Japanese poem that is still popular today is the *haiku*, a poem with only three lines. The words are chosen according to meaning and syllables. There are only seventeen syllables in the entire poem. A Japanese poet tries to create a mood and a picture with his words. Here are some modern examples of haikus that follow the ancient Japanese form.

Celebration

Leaves sprinkle the grass
Confetti tangled in hair.
Fall hosts a party.

Playground

Sloping string of grass
Droplets quiver at the top
To ride the green slide.

Japanese wood sculpture of Jizo Bosatsu created during the Heian period

To Write a Haiku

1. Get Notebook page 66, crayons, and a pencil.

2. Go to the playground and look at the things around you. What do you see? Select an object or scene. Describe it using a few creative words.

3. On Notebook page 66, describe your object or picture, using five syllables in the first line of the poem, seven syllables in the second line, and five syllables in the last line. The middle line should describe your scene, using a *metaphor,* a type of word symbol. Choose another object or scene. Write a haiku about it.

4. Illustrate one of your haikus.

The Arts

Even today, Japanese art and architecture resemble those of China. This influence began before the Heian period. The Japanese looked to China for models in painting, calligraphy, sculpture, and music.

Gradually, the Japanese left the Chinese models and developed their own artistic patterns. One characteristic of Japanese art was brilliant color. Bright colors made paintings full of life and activity. Colors decorated houses and temples as well. A second characteristic of Japanese art is its use of everyday objects. Boxes, baskets, furniture, combs, and fans were painted and carved. These objects were beautiful as well as useful.

Ikebana was a special Japanese art form that involved arranging flowers. Colors and types of flowers were chosen carefully to match the occasion and the season. Chrysanthemums, for example, were used in the month of May. Every year a Chrysanthemum Festival was held in which the emperor inspected the flower gardens at the palace. In celebration, the Japanese drank wine that was made from chrysanthemums, believing that the wine would give them a long life.

All the arts were important at court. Painters and sculptors represented court life in their works. Architects designed new buildings, and calligraphers recorded the writings of the court with their beautiful penmanship. Elegant music and graceful dancing entertained the people.

Japan

Location—A chain of islands in the Pacific Ocean east of China and Korea.

Climate—Varies from north to south. Average temperatures range from winter lows of 21°F in the north to summer highs of 79°F in the south. Annual precipitation is an average of fifty inches.

Topography—Four main islands and a large number of smaller islands that are really the peaks of submerged mountains. The Japanese Alps on the island of Honshu include Mount Fuji, Japan's highest mountain (12,388 feet). Many of the island mountains are volcanoes.

Natural Resources—Few natural resources. The mountainous terrain leaves less than 15 percent of land that can be farmed. Small deposits of coal, zinc, copper, lead, and gold may be found. The many short, swift rivers are used to provide electricity and to irrigate rice paddies.

Geography and Culture—Living on islands encouraged the Japanese people to use the sea for transportation and food. Japan's closeness to China allowed Chinese culture to influence Japan's art and religion.

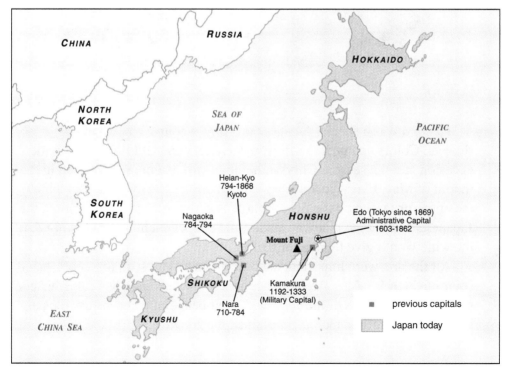

Gupta Empire about A.D. 400
tributary states

Indus River

Brahmaputra River

Godavari River

ARABIAN SEA

Bay of Bengal

India's Golden Years

Do you remember where Buddhism first started? In India. Look at a globe. It is easy to see how India, China, and Japan shared ideas, religions, and trade. India, like China and Japan, had its own golden age too. India's golden years were from A.D. 320 to 540.

In these years, India was ruled by a dynasty called the Gupta. The Gupta dynasty began in A.D. 320 under King Chandragupta. Beginning with a small kingdom, Chandragupta built an empire in northern India. Under his grandson, Chandragupta II, the Gupta Empire reached the peak of its golden age. During the Gupta dynasty, the Indians made great advances in science, art, and literature.

Student Life

The Gupta period was India's golden age of learning. A Hindu boy began his education at home where he learned the alphabet and *Sanskrit,* the Indian language. Once a boy reached a certain age, his family held a special *initiation* ceremony. A priest placed a special sacred cord on the boy's left shoulder and fastened it under his right arm. The cord had three strands, each one woven from nine threads. Throughout the rest of his life, the boy would wear the sacred cord as the symbol of his place in Hindu society.

Once this ceremony of the sacred cord was performed, the Hindu boy went to live with his teacher, who was called a *guru.* The guru began by teaching the student the ritual phrases he would repeat every day for the rest of his life.

A guru usually worked with several students at a time. They spent several hours a day learning the *Vedas,* sacred Hindu texts that were written in Sanskrit. In order to learn the *Vedas* perfectly, the boys memorized small phrases or verses. They repeated them forward and backward for the guru. Once the students had memorized the passages, the teacher lectured about the students' duties in society and the rules for living according to their *caste,* or social class.

The guru also taught his students Hindu rituals. Every activity from cooking a meal to fighting a battle followed a ritual. The Hindus believed that the correct performance of these rituals was necessary to please the Hindu gods.

Our Number System

Write the numerals one to ten on a piece of scrap paper. Think about the numerals around you—prices in the grocery store, the numerals on street signs, or the numerals in your textbook. Did you ever wonder where the numbers we use came from?

The Gupta age was the golden age of mathematics, science, and medicine. Many of these subjects that we use today echo the Indian achievements. What we call *Arabic* numerals were really invented by the Hindus. Arabic numerals are the numerals we use every day, such as *1, 2, 3,* and *4.* How are these numerals different from *Roman* numerals?

The Indians were also one of the first peoples to use a zero. Several hundred years before, the Mayas had invented zero, but the Indians discovered it independently. It is the zero invented in India that spread into Europe in the 1400s. The Indians also used the decimal system, place values, and positive and negative numbers. In more advanced mathematics, the Indians learned how to find square and cubic roots, figured an accurate value for *pi,* and used elementary algebra.

In science, Indian students studied chemistry, physics, and astronomy. Far ahead of other people living at this time, the Gupta Indians described the principle of gravity. They even had an idea of how atoms make up all matter.

Through their careful observations and calculations, they discovered that the earth and all planets are spheres. They also found that the earth rotates, and they calculated a nearly correct value for the earth's diameter. Many centuries passed before the Europeans accepted these ideas from the Indians.

In medicine, Indian students learned from dissecting human corpses. They also performed some surgeries and applied first aid.

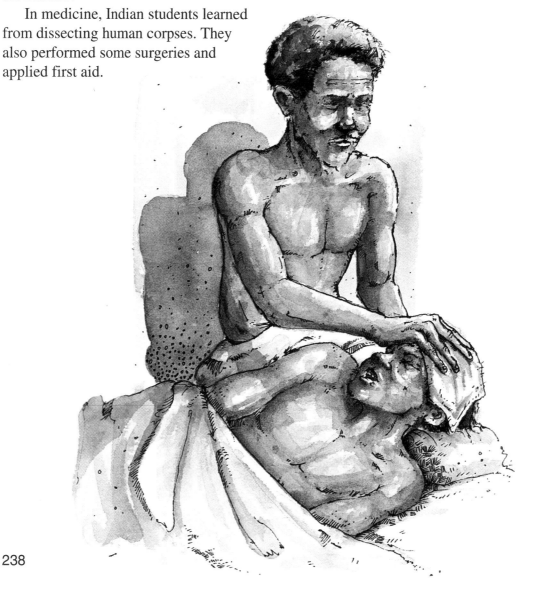

The Age of Literature

Besides science and math, Indian students studied the language arts: grammar, writing, and literature. They polished their writing of Sanskrit. They also studied the literature of India's finest dramatists and poets. Many excellent writers lived during the Gupta age. Their writings made this the golden age of Sanskrit literature.

Two types of literature that were popular during the Gupta age were the fable and the fairy tale. Indian fables and fairy tales were popular not only in India but also in other countries. How do you think other countries first came in contact with Indian literature? Trade had a big part in spreading the stories that Indian writers created.

Many of the traditional stories that we have today are based on the early fables of India. One such story is that of Sinbad the Sailor in *A Thousand and One Nights*. Indian poetry, on the other hand, did not spread like the fables. The poetry of this time was complex and a favorite pastime of the people of the court. The ability to create poetry was very important; competitions were often held to see who could write the best and most complicated poem.

Gentlemanly Pursuits

During the Gupta period, a gentleman had to have a knowledge of art and music. If he showed any ability in this area, he tried to develop it.

The Indians of the Gupta period produced such excellent works that this age is called the *Classical Age* of Indian art or music. Indian music was not like the music we hear today. It was not even like what we call classical music. Most Indian music was not written down. A performer began with a familiar tune and then improvised, or made changes in the melody as he played.

The main instrument that the Indians used was called a *vina*. The vina was a type of lute similar to a guitar. They also played flutes and other reed instruments. Drums, bells, cymbals, and gongs were other common Indian instruments. Trumpets, made from large conch shells, were used only for battle or other special occasions.

Playing the vina

Gupta Art

The art of the Gupta appears peaceful and happy. Many of the best examples of Indian sculpture come from this period. The wealthy enjoyed painting. Most gentlemen and ladies knew how to paint. Many people had their own private galleries of both their own works and the works of others. In the cities, public galleries displayed artwork for the poorer people.

The best examples of Gupta paintings that we have today are found in the caves at *Ajanta*. These paintings were done by Buddhist artists. Although they are primarily scenes from the life of Buddha, the paintings include details of Indian life. From these paintings we can learn something of how the people lived, such as what they wore and what plants and animals they raised.

This detail shows two seated Buddhas from a wall painting found in the Ajanta Caves, Maharashtra, India (Gupta period, 5th-6th century).

During the golden age of the Orient, life for the people of China, Japan, and India was changing and improving. New inventions and ideas affected all areas of society—medicine, mathematics, literature, poetry, art, architecture, and even religion.

Time tests the success of man, however. As the years slipped by, these great societies began to lose their glitter. Wars and fightings caused the great dynasties to crumble and fall.

Today China is governed by Communism. The Chinese people suffer great restrictions under its rule. In India there is fighting between the Hindus and Muslims. The Indian people suffer many hardships from drought and poverty. Of the three countries, Japan is the most successful. The Japanese economy is prospering with the manufacturing of cars, machines, and electronic devices. Japan's trade with other countries has greatly added to this success, but the people must deal with stress, overcrowded cities, and pollution.

Throughout history, the civilizations of the Orient moved in cycles of failure to success to failure. Perhaps the modern countries of China, Japan, and India will reach a golden peak once more in the course of time; yet, without God, neither they nor any other nation can ever reach true success.

"Verily every man at his best state is altogether vanity."

Psalm 39:5

Mosaics and Minarets:
Byzantine Empire

"Who cares about this old empire?" Dan rested his head on his hands.

"I don't know, but I'm out of here in an hour," said Troy. He punched the inside of his baseball glove. "Coach wants me to set up the bases for practice. So let's get this report over with. What's the first question? Give it to me—I like fast balls."

Dan tossed the baseball across the table. He picked up the sheet of paper as the ball slapped into Troy's glove. "How did the Byzantine Empire get its name?"

Troy pulled his book over. He ran his finger down the paragraph. "Here it is. The empire was named after the village Byzantium. Write that down, Dan."

"We'd better find that on the map. You know how Miss Hayden is about geography." Dan studied his textbook. "Here it is. Right there by the southwest corner of the Black Sea . . . on the Straits of the Bosporus, that real narrow body of water right there." He pointed and held the book under Troy's nose.

The Village by the Sea

Greek colonists from Athens built the village of Byzantium where the Black Sea flows into the Straits of the Bosporus across from Asia Minor. This was an ideal place for a village. The triangle-shaped piece of land had water on two sides, and the Athenians built a wall across the land side to make their village safe.

This location was also good for trade. A fine harbor lay just north of the village. Villagers could travel around the Black Sea to trade with Asian merchants who had brought furs and amber down the Dnieper and Don Rivers, or they could sail west into the Aegean and Mediterranean Seas. There they could trade with the Greeks, Romans, and North Africans for grain, gold, and ivory.

Merchants came overland from India and China with silks and spices to sell. Their caravans traveled through Asia Minor and crossed the straits at the narrowest point, right where Byzantium had been built. The Byzantine villagers saw almost everything anyone had to sell.

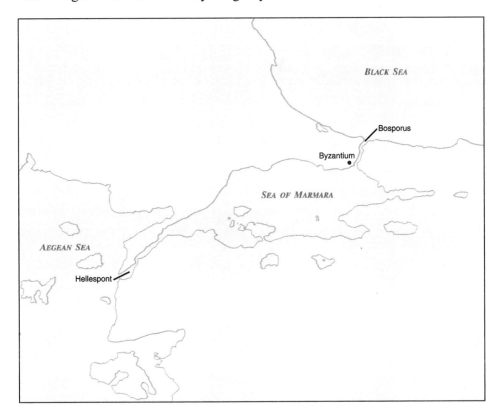

Turkey

Location—Turkey, once part of the Byzantine Empire, is in southeastern Europe and Anatolia (Asia Minor).

Climate—Temperate along the coast; harsh and dry on the plateau; snowy or icy in the mountains. Average temperatures range from 13°F to 80°F.

Topography—Has an inland plateau formed by the Taurus and Pontic mountain ranges. In eastern Turkey, where these two chains meet, is Mount Ararat.

Natural Resources—Has large mineral deposits, but most have not been mined. Oil has been discovered and is now being produced.

Geography and Culture—Situated on the southern bridge between Europe and Asia, the region has been conquered many times and has a mixed cultural heritage.

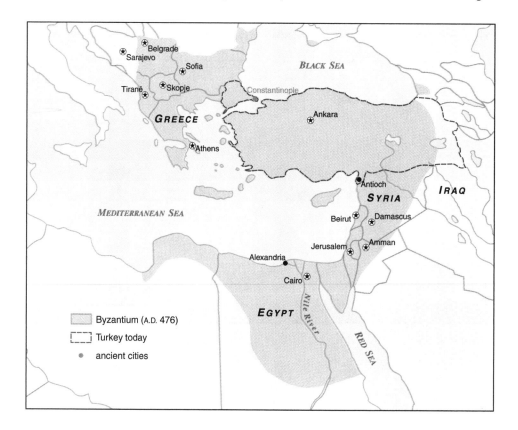

"Wish I'd been there," said Dan. "Just think of all that neat stuff you could trade for. Wonder what they'd give you for baseball cards? I'd get rich and live like a king."

"Not at first." Troy kept reading. "It says here that Byzantium did not grow rapidly. When the Roman emperor Constantine saw the village, he knew it could become a great city, so he built a new city right where the old village had been. He named it Constantinople, after himself."

Constantinople during the Byzantine Era, around 1493

Constantine's new city became one of the greatest cities of the world. It was a secure place, far away from the wars and invasions among the barbarians in other parts of Europe. *Barbarian* was a name given by the Romans to nomadic peoples who had not adopted Roman culture and who did not speak Latin or Greek. The Romans considered these people primitive and crude. By A.D. 470 the Roman emperors had moved to Constantinople. Now the emperors were too far away to protect the western half of their empire. The barbarians soon controlled all of western Europe.

Early Years of the Byzantine Empire

Justinian I, the first great emperor of Byzantium, reigned from 527 to 565. But he wanted to rule more than the eastern half of the old Roman Empire. He sent his best warrior, General Belisarius, to reconquer the western provinces.

Belisarius first conquered Egypt, an important grain-producing province. Then he marched his army across North Africa to the city of Carthage. A barbarian people called the Vandals ruled there. They were fierce fighters, but Belisarius's army defeated them and destroyed their kingdom.

Next, Belisarius's men built ships so that they could cross the Mediterranean Sea and invade the island of Sicily. Before long, the general led his army through Italy and claimed it for Emperor Justinian. Justinian now controlled land on what three continents?

Compare the map of the old Roman Empire with the map of the new Byzantine Empire. Did Justinian get his wish to rule all of the old Roman Empire? What parts of the Roman Empire did Belisarius not conquer?

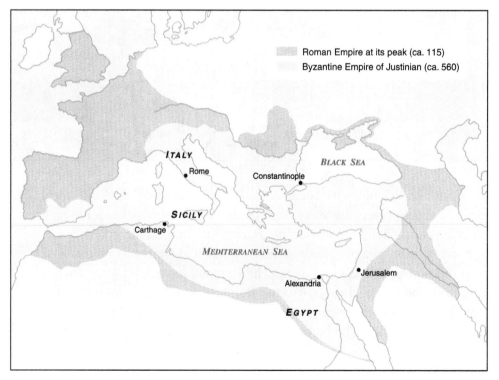

Roman Empire at its peak (ca. 115)
Byzantine Empire of Justinian (ca. 560)

ITALY
Rome
BLACK SEA
Constantinople
SICILY
Carthage
MEDITERRANEAN SEA
Jerusalem
Alexandria
EGYPT

Corpus Juris Civilis

Justinian believed that a reunited, well-governed empire needed a good system of law. He adopted all the laws of the old Roman Empire. Imagine how many laws had been passed in the last five hundred years! When you add to that all the lawyers' opinions about the laws, there must have been enough books to fill a city library. No one could learn all the law.

Tribonia, a member of the court, was chosen to simplify the law and to make it easy to understand. In just four years, he and his committee finished their work.

The new, much shorter law code was called the *Corpus Juris Civilis,* or *The Body of Civil Law.* Because of this work, we know a great deal about Roman law. And some modern European countries, such as France and Italy, base their legal systems on this law code.

Not everything went smoothly for Justinian. Two great sports clubs in the city of Constantinople were the cause of his problems. These clubs were called the Greens and the Blues. Almost everyone in the city belonged to one of these clubs. At sporting events, they cheered their favorite teams to victory.

These clubs also served as the city guard and helped keep the city walls in repair. When they disagreed with the government, they rioted. In 532, the Greens and the Blues protested the emperor's high taxes. During these *Nika Riots,* the club members looted and burned much of the city.

Justinian would have run for his life had it not been for his wife, Theodora. She had been a circus performer before she married Justinian. She told her husband that she preferred to die an empress and that royal purple made a fine shroud. Justinian found enough courage to stay and sent Belisarius out to fight the rioters.

Belisarius waited until the Blues and the Greens were holding a meeting in the *hippodrome,* a large open-air stadium, and then he led his army in. At the end of the battle, thousands of rioters lay dead in the huge arena.

The Hippodrome in Constantinople

Troy leaned across the table. "Can you believe that? Sports clubs leading riots! Coach would make us do pushups for fifty years if we acted that way."

Dan tapped his book with the eraser of his pencil. "And that part about Theodora. An emperor marrying a *circus performer?*"

"I didn't believe it, either. But Miss Hayden says that Theodora was a circus performer, and Justinian was the son of a peasant."

"How'd they get to be the rulers?"

"Justinian's uncle was emperor before him and made Justinian his heir."

"No wonder Justinian was scared—he was brand-new at this emperor thing. Let's see what else he did."

Taxes went up even more after the Nika Riots because so much of the city needed to be rebuilt. Justinian took advantage of the opportunity to make Constantinople more beautiful than it had ever been. The emperor set his architects to work, planning and building new public baths, government buildings, churches, and aqueducts and cisterns for carrying and storing water.

The most famous of all these structures was the *Hagia Sophia,* or the Church of Holy Wisdom. The Hagia Sophia was the most important and most beautiful church in the empire. It still stands today.

The church was built in the form of a Greek cross, which is a cross that has arms of equal length. Over the center of the church, the builders erected a magnificent dome that reached 184 feet above the floor. The Ottoman Turks added the *minarets,* the four surrounding towers, to the Hagia Sophia after 1453.

The inside of the Hagia Sophia was brilliantly decorated. A picture of God the Father surrounded by angels and archangels looked down from the highest part of the dome. Pictures of the saints covered the walls of the church. Many of these pictures were *mosaics.* Mosaics are pictures made of small stones or pieces of glass set in mortar. Have you ever seen a mosaic?

Hagia Sophia (below) and a mosaic from its interior (right)

To Make a Mosaic

1. Get glue, scissors, and several different-colored sheets of construction paper.

2. Cut the construction paper into small squares or shapes of varying sizes.

3. Apply a thin layer of glue to a small portion of a sheet of construction paper.

4. Arrange the small pieces of paper close together, side by side on top of the glue. Keep working, applying glue and arranging pieces to form a picture, until the entire sheet of paper is covered and no more glue can be seen.

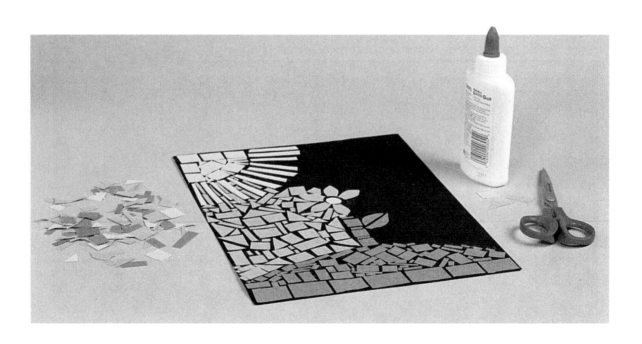

The Empire's Struggle for Existence

After rebuilding the city, the emperors had no money left in the imperial treasury. To save money, they decreased their soldiers' pay.

The soldiers in the Byzantine army were foreigners hired by the government. They came from many countries, were paid to fight, and were loyal only to their generals. Such soldiers were called *mercenaries.* If you were a mercenary, what would you do if the Byzantine emperor paid you only half of what he had promised?

The Persian emperor thought this would be a good time to attack the Byzantine Empire and take Syria for himself. He wanted Syria because it was rich from trade and could afford to pay high taxes. The Byzantine emperor did not want to lose Syria. Because the mercenary armies would not fight for half pay, the Persians won the war.

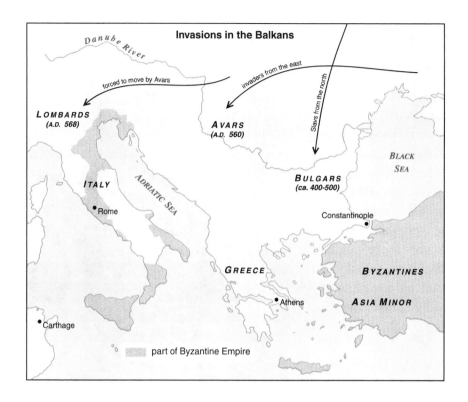

Invasions in the Balkans

Danube River

forced to move by Avars

invaders from the east

Slavs from the north

LOMBARDS
(A.D. 568)

AVARS
(A.D. 560)

BLACK
SEA

ITALY

ADRIATIC SEA

BULGARS
(ca. 400-500)

• Rome

Constantinople
•

GREECE

BYZANTINES

ASIA MINOR

• Athens

• Carthage

part of Byzantine Empire

The Byzantine armies did not fight well in the Balkans either. Can you find the Balkan region on the map? Line a ruler up from the north end of the Adriatic Sea to the northwest corner of the Black Sea. All the land to the south, including Greece but not Asia Minor, is the Balkan Region.

Two barbarian tribes from Asia were migrating into this area. They were called the Avars and the Bulgars. They were strong enough to take the land away from Byzantium and settle in it.

Then the emperor received news of another tribe of barbarians called the Lombards. They had invaded Italy and had successfully attacked the empire there. In just one hundred years, Byzantium lost nearly all the land conquered by Justinian's general, Belisarius. The Byzantine Empire seemed to be disappearing from the map.

Heraclius

Heraclius began his reign in A.D. 610. Without him the Byzantine Empire might have disappeared. He reformed the army, reconquered the land taken by Persia and the barbarians, and made the roads safe for commerce.

To reform the army, Heraclius fired the mercenary soldiers and trained Byzantine peasants for the army. Heraclius did not have enough money to pay his new citizen-soldiers, so he gave each one enough land to support himself and his family.

With his new army, Heraclius drove the Persians from Asia Minor and conquered Syria, Palestine, and Egypt. Then he marched the army to the Balkans and defeated the Avars. Why do you think these citizen-soldiers were more successful than the mercenaries?

Heraclius added so much land to the empire that he had to find a new way to organize it. He divided the land into provinces called *themes*. Each theme was a military zone with many peasant soldiers living in it. These soldiers were responsible for the theme's defense. This system lasted almost until the fall of the Byzantine Empire in 1453.

Trade flourished under the government of Heraclius. Special groups called *guilds* united moneychangers, goldsmiths, and notaries, who oversaw the writing of legal documents. In the cities, other guilds supplied meat, fish, and bread to the populace. Foreign merchants traveled throughout Byzantium selling furs, leather, slaves, wax, ointments, spices, and grain.

One of the most important items of trade was silk. Silk was worn only by the members of the government. Each government official had his insignia of office woven into the fabric. Silk was extremely expensive because it came all the way from China, and the Persians controlled much of the silk trade route.

Byzantine spies discovered how the Chinese made silk. They stole some silkworms and smuggled them out of China. Silk production became one of the most important industries in the empire, especially in the cities of Constantinople, Antioch, Tyre, and Beirut.

Chinese workers collecting silkworm cocoons to use in making silk

Heraclius also changed the language of the empire. Though the people of Byzantium believed their empire was a continuation of the old Roman Empire, very few Byzantines in the seventh century spoke Latin. Almost everyone spoke Greek, so Heraclius decreed that the language of the empire would be Greek. He even stopped using Roman titles for emperor and used the Greek title *Basilius.*

Dan rubbed his eyes. "I didn't think I'd like studying the Byzantine Empire very much. Heraclius was some emperor!"

"Look at the next question," Troy said. "'What new empire threatened the Byzantine Empire during the seventh century?' Seems like this empire was always getting into fights with somebody! Man, all this competition stuff is putting me in the mood for baseball!" He tossed the ball to Dan.

A New Enemy and a New Faith

Far to the south, in the city of Mecca, a merchant named Muhammad was concerned for his people, the Arabs. They had no government or system of law to guarantee peace.

Muhammad traveled throughout the Middle East. Along the caravan routes, he met people from all over the world. Persians told him of the greatness of their empire and its laws. Jewish merchants explained their faith in the *Torah.* The Torah gave them the laws they lived by. The Christian merchants declared that God had given all people the Bible to tell them of the freedom offered in Christ.

Muhammad wanted his people to have a holy book of their own. One day, he claimed that he had received a special message from the angel Gabriel. Gabriel told Muhammad that Allah had chosen him to be his prophet. Through Muhammad, Allah would give the Arab people a holy book that would tell them how to live without fighting.

Allah's holy book was called the *Koran.* Muslims believed that the Koran contained the messages given to Muhammad from Allah. The new religion was called *Islam. Islam* means "submission to Allah." Anyone who followed Islam was called a *Muslim,* or one who submits to Allah. Those who did not believe were called *infidels.*

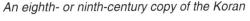

An eighth- or ninth-century copy of the Koran

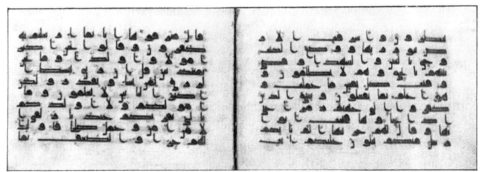

The Kaaba

This craftsman is working on part of a gold- and silver-embroidered cloth to cover the Kaaba. A new cover is made each year at a cost of several million dollars.

Muhammad preached this new religion on the street corners of Mecca. What do you think the people of Mecca thought of these new ideas? The Meccans did not like the new religion because it had only one god. Their old religion had many gods. And in Mecca stood a temple where many of the idols of those gods were kept. Every year thousands of Arabs came to worship at this temple called the *Kaaba.* If the Arab people accepted Muhammad's new religion, the merchants of Mecca were afraid they would lose all the money that came from the yearly *pilgrimage.*

In the year 622, the non-Muslim Meccans forced Muhammad to leave his home. He led his followers two hundred miles north to the city of Medina. Their flight from Mecca was called the *Hegira.* The year of the Hegira, 622, is the first year of the Islamic calendar.

The city of Medina welcomed Muhammad because he helped settle serious disagreements between some of the city's families. The Medinans soon made Muhammad their governor, but Muhammad was still thinking of Mecca. He wanted the Meccans to accept the new religion of Islam. He also believed that the Kaaba was the sacred temple of Allah. He and his followers wanted to worship there. How do you think he accomplished these goals?

In the year 630, Muhammad led his army to Mecca. When an Islamic army fights for its faith, the war is called a *jihad,* or holy war. The Muslims conquered the city and went directly to the Kaaba. There Muhammad removed all the idols and declared it the temple of Allah. The jihad against Mecca had been successful, and the city accepted Islam.

The Conquests of the Muslims

The men who led the Muslims after Muhammad's death were called *caliphs* or successors. Many of them were fine generals. The first was Abu-Bakr. He led the Muslim army into the Arabian Peninsula. In only two years he conquered the whole peninsula and converted its people to Islam.

No one could stop the Muslim army. Caliph Omar's best general, Khalid ibn al-Walid, led the army into Persia. After defeating one of the Persian armies, Caliph Omar sent his army against Syria and Egypt and captured both from Heraclius, emperor of Byzantium. How could Omar's army succeed against the two powerful empires of Persia and Byzantium?

Persia had been fighting Byzantium for a long time, and by the time Omar's army reached Persia, the Persian soldiers were exhausted. The Byzantine soldiers were weary too. In addition to fighting the Persians in the southeast, Heraclius's army had been fighting the Avars and Bulgars in the Balkans. The Byzantine army simply was not large enough to fight the Arabs at the same time.

During these battles, Khalid conquered Jerusalem, where the Muslims wanted to worship at a sacred rock. The Dome of the Rock, an Islamic mosque, stands over the rock today.

The Dome of the Rock is built on the spot in Jerusalem believed to be the site of Muhammad's ascension into heaven.

259

Conflict Continues

To provide soldiers for all their wars, the Byzantine emperors gave more and more land to peasants who joined the army. The nobility especially disliked this practice. They thought only noblemen should own land. The wars also brought a rise in taxes and angered the Byzantines. Often rebellion resulted, and the current emperor was murdered.

For twenty years civil war tore the empire. Seven emperors tried to rule during this time. Most were assassinated after only a few months on the throne. The empire needed a powerful ruler to save it.

Leo the Isaurian was the man they needed. He could handle all the problems of the empire. He had lived among the Arabs when he was a boy. He even spoke Arabic. When he was older, his family had moved to the Balkan area, so he was familiar with the barbarians there.

As an adult, Leo had served as an administrator and a general in the Byzantine government. Soon he was more powerful than the emperor. With his army, Leo captured the emperor and all his household. In A.D. 717 he named himself Emperor Leo III.

Muslim ships burning from Greek fire

Just six months after Leo became emperor, Muslim armies camped outside the walls of Constantinople. The Muslim navy closed off the city by sea. They were trying to starve the citizens into surrendering.

Leo III sent his ships out against the Muslims. The Byzantines had only a few ships, but they had something even more important—a secret weapon. They had invented an explosive mixture called *Greek fire* that burst into flames when it touched water. When the Muslim ships drew close enough, the defenders of Constantinople threw their Greek fire toward the ships. The Muslim ships burned to the water line. Then Leo could bring supplies into his city by ship so that no one would starve.

The following winter was so cold that many of the Muslim soldiers encamped around Constantinople froze to death. The next summer a large number died of a plague. Finally, the Muslims withdrew. Leo led his army into Asia Minor and took it back from the Muslims.

Leo had proved his ability to lead the empire. However, he believed that he ruled not only the empire but also the church. Claiming to have authority over both the state and the church is called *caesaropapism.* Can you see the two parts of this word? A *caesar* rules the state. A pope, or *papal* government, rules the church. Leo III was a caesaropapist.

Troy shoved his book across the table. "Look at that picture. That's an actual picture of Greek fire. I wonder what it's made of?"

Dan shrugged and frowned. "I'm confused," he said. "Are Muslims the same as Arabs?"

Troy was still looking at the picture of the burning ships. "Huh? Oh, it's simple. The Arabs were the people of Muhammad. Islam is the religion Muhammad invented for the Arabs. Arabs who believed in Islam were called Muslims."

"So the Arab army and Muslim army are the same army."

"Yeah." Troy turned back to his book. "I want to find out more about this Greek fire."

Iconoclasm

Icons are sacred pictures and statues of Jesus and the saints. When an earthquake shook Constantinople in 726, Leo believed it was a judgment from God against the use of icons. He ordered the destruction of all sacred statues and pictures in the churches.

Hatred of icons is called iconoclasm. Throughout the empire, those who disliked icons, called *iconoclasts,* broke statues and painted over pictures.

Many people, however, tried to protect the icons. These people appealed to Pope Gregory III in Rome. The pope believed that he, not Leo, was the head of the church. He thought it was right to use icons in worshiping God. The pope condemned what Leo had done.

Leo was not going to allow the pope in faraway Rome to tell him how to govern the Byzantine Empire. He imprisoned those who tried to protect the icons, including some messengers from the pope.

Neither Leo III nor Pope Gregory III was going to give in. Finally, the church divided between Byzantium in the East and Rome in the West. This same division exists today. The eastern part is called the Eastern Orthodox Church. Its leader is called the *patriarch.* The western part is called the Roman Catholic Church and is controlled by the pope.

Iconoclasm ended in the year 843. But the division of the church between the East and West remained.

Byzantine 13th Century, Madonna and Child on a Curved Throne, *Andrew W. Mellon Collection, Image © 2006 Board of Trustees, National Gallery of Art, Washington.*

> *"Thou shalt not make unto thee any graven image, or any likeness of any thing that is in heaven above, or that is in the earth beneath, or that is in the water under the earth."*
>
> *Exodus 20:4*

The Golden Age of the Byzantine Empire

The empire had its best and most powerful years between 843 and 1025. The emperors successfully fought their enemies in the Balkans and the Middle East. Michael III reorganized the University of Constantinople. Basil I oversaw the revision of the law. The empire became more and more wealthy from its trade throughout Asia, Europe, and Africa.

Missionaries traveled throughout eastern Europe. Two missionaries, Cyril and Methodius, translated the Bible into Slavic. Because the Slavic people did not have a written language, the missionaries had to invent a new alphabet. They called it the Cyrillic alphabet. Because of the work of these two missionaries, thousands of people learned of the gospel of Christ.

The most unusual emperor during the golden age was Basil II. He never married, and he devoted his life to making the empire stronger. His army was well trained, and he made the nobles collect his taxes. He kept the church from taking land from the peasants. Though Basil was somber and suspicious, he was one of the fairest and best rulers the Byzantine Empire ever had.

Cyrillic Alphabet		
Russian		Roman equivalent
А	а	a
Б	б	b
В	в	v
Г	г	g
Д	д	d
Е	е	ye
Ё	ё	yo
Ж	ж	zh
З	з	z
И	и	i
Й	й	y
К	к	k
Л	л	l
М	м	m
Н	н	n
О	о	o
П	п	p
Р	р	r
С	с	s
Т	т	t
У	у	u
Ф	ф	f
Х	х	kh
Ц	ц	ts
Ч	ч	ch
Ш	ш	sh
Щ	щ	shsh
Ъ	ъ	—
Ы	ы	y
ь	ь	—
Э	э	e
Ю	ю	yu
Я	я	ya

Basil II, often called "the Bulgar Slayer," was a great warrior. When the Bulgars attacked the empire, Basil not only defeated them but also captured fourteen thousand of their soldiers. To intimidate the Bulgar king, he blinded all the captured soldiers and sent them back home in groups of a hundred. Each group had a one-eyed man to lead the way. When the Bulgar king saw his soldiers blinded and stumbling, he reportedly fell over dead. How many other kings do you suppose would challenge Basil after they heard this story?

The Crusader Kingdom of Constantinople

After Basil II's death, no one was strong enough to run the government the way he had. The empire weakened, both inside and out. Venice, an Italian city, took over much of the trade. New enemies appeared: the Normans from northern Europe, the Patzinaks from Russia, and the Seljuk Turks from central Asia. All of them attacked the empire. The Byzantines hated the Turks most of all because the Turks had captured the holy city of Jerusalem.

In 1096, Emperor Alexius Comnenus I sent a message to the pope in Rome, asking for help to fight the Turks. He needed a well-trained army of professional soldiers. Instead, Pope Urban II called all the knights in Europe to a crusade against the Turks. Their effort was called the First Crusade.

Thousands of knights prepared for the long march to Constantinople. They were going to rescue Byzantium, but it would be even better, they thought, to rescue Jerusalem. The crusaders forgot about helping the emperor and went right on to Jerusalem.

Alexius never did get the army for which he had asked. Neither he nor the emperors who ruled after him could win back the territory that had been lost. By the year 1200, the Turks controlled the Middle East from Egypt to Syria.

About one hundred years later, in the year 1202, Pope Innocent III called for a special crusade. He told the knights they would be going to Egypt to fight the Turkish leader Saladin. But he really wanted the crusaders to fight Byzantium. He wanted to reunite the Eastern Orthodox Church with the Roman Catholic Church. This was called the Fourth Crusade.

The Venetians provided ships to take the knights across the Mediterranean Sea. During the voyage they told the knights about the wealth of Constantinople. "You'll become rich," they told the crusaders. "And after you help us in Constantinople, you can go on to Egypt and fight Saladin if you'd like."

The knights argued for several weeks. Finally, they agreed to help. The Venetians sailed their ships into the Aegean Sea toward Constantinople. Many historians wonder whether the Venetians ever meant to take the crusaders to Egypt at all. What do you think?

When the ships reached Constantinople, they broke the great floating barrier that barred the entry to the city's harbor, the *Golden Horn.* The Venetian ships attacked from the sea while the crusaders attacked the city walls from the land.

Constantinople fell. The emperor fled, taking with him the imperial treasure and the crown jewels. On April 13, 1204, the crusaders and Venetians took over the government. For three days, the soldiers and sailors killed thousands of people and destroyed many priceless treasures. A Byzantine writer said that even the Turks were more merciful and kind than the men "who bear the cross of Christ on their shoulders."

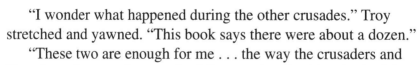

"I wonder what happened during the other crusades." Troy stretched and yawned. "This book says there were about a dozen."

"These two are enough for me . . . the way the crusaders and Venetians destroyed so much of Constantinople. They both claimed to be Christian, but they sure didn't act like it. I wonder what Saladin, the Muslim leader, thought about that."

"Yeah." Troy turned the baseball over and over in his hand. "It's kind of the same way in sports. The other teams know we're a Christian school. Wonder what they think of us?"

The Recovery of Byzantium

The crusaders never did go on to Egypt to fight Saladin. From 1204 to 1261 the Venetians and crusaders ruled Constantinople. It looked as if the Byzantine Empire had come to an end.

But the real government of Byzantium had not been destroyed. The Byzantines fled to Asia Minor where they organized a new empire. Nicaea was its capital. For over fifty-seven years the new empire fought the armies of both Constantinople and the Turks.

The emperors at Nicaea worked hard to strengthen their new state. One emperor, John III, banned evil practices in government and the courts. He helped the poor by founding hospitals and charitable institutions. His government built churches and gave land to its citizen-soldiers. The government also encouraged the improvement of agriculture and raising stock. To protect his people, the emperor had a system of fortifications and frontier defenses built.

By 1261, Emperor Michael VIII had strengthened his army enough to attack and capture Constantinople. He entered the old capital of Byzantium on August 15, 1261, and was recrowned emperor in the Hagia Sophia the following September. Michael VIII spent vast sums of money to rebuild and beautify his capital.

The Decline and Fall of the Byzantine Empire

Michael VIII tried to win back the rest of the land held by the former Byzantine Empire. But a new group of Turks, called the Ottomans, had invaded the Middle East. The Ottoman Turks conquered the Seljuk Turks, adopted Islam as their religion, and moved north to attack Byzantium.

The Ottomans threatened the empire in Asia Minor, and the Serbs attacked in the Balkans. Since Michael VIII did not have enough money to go to war, he divided the empire among his family members, hoping that each would protect his share. But his relatives all wanted to make their parts of the empire independent little countries. They each hired mercenaries and were soon fighting each other instead of protecting the empire.

Meanwhile, Venetian and Genoese merchants gained control of Constantinople's trade. They collected the profits and taxes from commerce that had once belonged to the emperor. The emperors became so poor that they had to sell their gold and silver dishes and the palace decorations to pay their bills.

By 1371 the Turks had conquered all of the Byzantine Empire except the city of Constantinople. Some Byzantine emperors visited Europe, hoping to find a king who would send an army to fight the Ottoman Turks. The leaders of the Eastern Orthodox Church begged the pope in Rome for help for the empire. Do you think he was willing to help them?

This silver plate showing David's being anointed by Samuel is one of a series of David Plates from Constantinople (A.D. 613-629/30).

The Metropolitan Museum of Art, Gift of J. Pierpont Morgan, 1917 (17.190.398) Photograph © 1990 The Metropolitan Museum of Art

No one in Europe could help the Byzantines, even if he had been willing. All of Europe was suffering from the Black Death, a horrible disease that we now call the bubonic plague. The disease killed at least one-third of all the people in Europe. And England and France had been at war for over one hundred years. No ruler had an army or even money to help Byzantium.

After the Ottomans completed their conquest of Asia Minor, they crossed into the Balkans. The city of Adrianople and the country of Bulgaria fell to them, and then they conquered Greece. By March 1453 the Ottomans surrounded Constantinople. The last emperor, Constantine XI, died defending his city. After the battle his body could be identified only by the purple boots he wore.

Muhammad II's Muslim army destroyed or stole the priceless works of art, icons, and precious manuscripts of Constantinople, and then 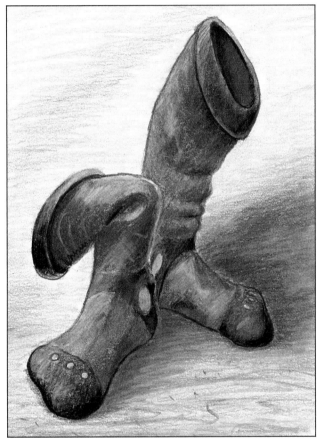 the Sultan solemnly entered the city and made it the capital of the Ottoman Empire. The beautiful Hagia Sophia became an Islamic mosque. The Byzantine Empire had come to an end.

Why was the Byzantine Empire important? The Byzantines kept Roman law from disappearing. The scholars of the empire preserved Greek literature, learning, and philosophy. Without the Byzantine Empire, much of what we study today about the ancient world would have been lost.

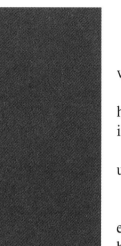

"Hey, Troy, look at the time!" Dan said.

"I can't believe it! I sure never thought studying the Byzantines would go that fast."

"Remember how all those Byzantines played sports? It said they had archery, javelin throwing, wrestling, and chariot racing. I'll bet if there were Byzantines around today, they'd love baseball."

"Yeah, too bad." Troy slammed his book shut. "Our team could use some more good players."

"You know what Coach would say about that. Good is an attitude."

"Yeah. You're right. Coach is always saying attitude's the hardest part." He studied his glove for a minute. "If all those crusaders had had better attitudes, things would have turned out better for the Byzantines."

Dan grabbed his glove. "I never thought something Coach said would turn up in our history books. Come on, let's go set up those bases."

Shadow of the Castle:
Middle Ages

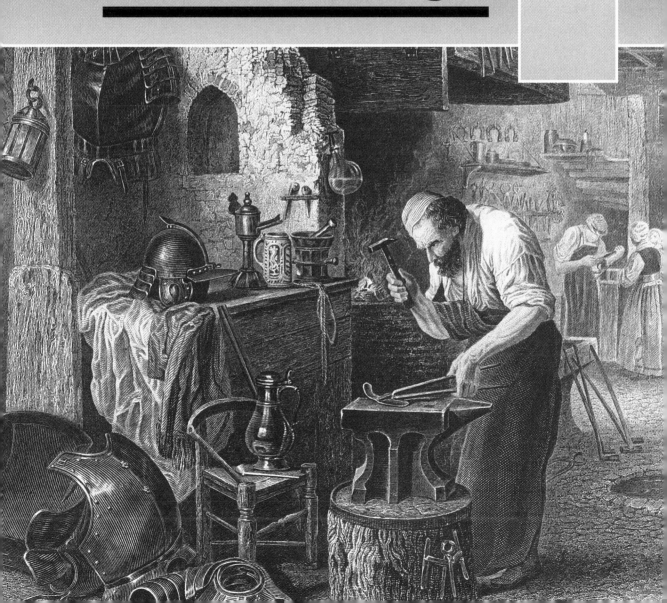

On a hill in France stands a deserted castle, its massive stone towers lifting to the sky. It seems to be listening for old sounds. The rustle of a lady's silk dress. The clank of a shield against a breastplate. Distant echoes of horses' hooves cantering off to battle. The hoarse voice of a serf, humming as he works out in the lord's field. Sounds that belonged to a different world.

After the fall of the Roman Empire, Europe was known for more than ten centuries as the medieval world. The word *medieval* comes from two Latin words—*medius,* meaning "middle" and *aevum,* meaning "age." Many people also call this time period between the fall of Rome and the Renaissance the Middle Ages.

Haut Konigsbourg, France

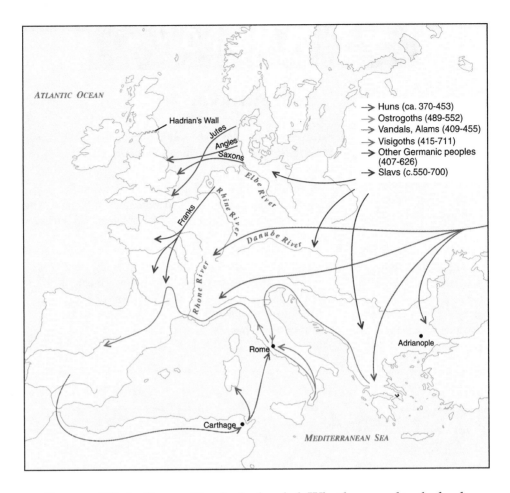

By A.D. 476, the Roman Empire had ended. What happened to the lands that had been part of Rome? The eastern half of this fallen empire eventually became the Byzantine Empire.

The western half was taken over by Germanic peoples from Scandinavia. A tribe called the *Visigoths* fought their way into Spain. The *Ostrogoths* set up a kingdom in Italy. The Franks conquered Gaul; and the Angles, the Saxons, and the Jutes invaded the British Isles.

When Rome fell apart, civilized life in most of Europe disappeared. Roads became overgrown with weeds, trade stopped, and cities stood in ruins. People built isolated villages and worked hard to grow enough food to feed their families. Disorder and destruction by invaders were constant threats to the people. No one had much time or money for education.

The people of the former Roman Empire needed a place to turn for leadership. Without an emperor to guide them, many turned to the church.

Scandinavia

Location—A group of countries surrounding the Baltic Sea in northern Europe: Denmark, Finland, Norway, and Sweden. The island of Iceland is also considered part of Scandinavia.

Climate—Temperate in the south to icy in the north, with temperatures ranging from 0°F to 60°F.

Topography—Low and flat in Denmark; mountainous in Norway and Sweden; low hills and mountains in Finland, with many lakes and rivers. Deep fjords, narrow inlets from the sea, are found along Norway's coast.

Geography and Culture—Because of the lack of farmland, most early Scandinavians either left their homeland or became seafarers.

Natural Resources—Forests cover much of Scandinavia's land, and large quantities of iron ore are buried beneath it. Oil and natural gas have been found in the North Sea.

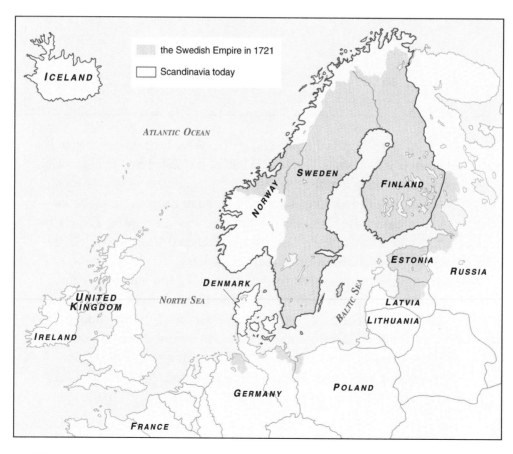

the Swedish Empire in 1721

Scandinavia today

ICELAND

ATLANTIC OCEAN

SWEDEN

NORWAY

FINLAND

ESTONIA

RUSSIA

DENMARK

NORTH SEA

BALTIC SEA

LATVIA

LITHUANIA

UNITED KINGDOM

IRELAND

GERMANY

POLAND

FRANCE

The bishop of the church of Rome was called the *pope,* a word that comes from the Latin word for "father." He soon extended his leadership over the whole Roman Church in Europe, not just the church in Rome. Europeans everywhere followed his teachings.

The pope directed the activities of the *clergy,* the religious leaders, during the Middle Ages. Two types of clergy worked in the Roman Church.

Some clergymen lived among the people. They ministered as priests in the churches. They led the services and instructed the people in how to live and worship. The priests of the Roman Church taught the people that they could not receive God's grace without the help of a priest. They also taught that people had to participate in certain ceremonies, called *sacraments,* in order to be saved. How do the priests' teachings compare to what the Bible says?

Medieval priests of the Roman Church

"For there is one God, and one mediator between God and men, the man Christ Jesus."

I Timothy 2:5

"For by grace are ye saved through faith; and that not of yourselves: it is the gift of God: Not of works, lest any man should boast."

Ephesians 2:8-9

Other clergymen, called *monks,* lived together in large quarters, or *monasteries,* and rarely had contact with the outside world. They vowed never to marry but instead to devote their lives to serving the Roman Church. What do you think made men want to live this sort of life?

Monasteries were among the few places where education was valued during the early Middle Ages. Literature, science, mathematics, and medicine were not often taught, but monks learned to read and write. Then they spent hours copying the Scriptures and the writings of the early churchmen. They copied by hand, bent for hours at a time over their writing desks, checking each word of the original manuscripts against the scratchings of their quill pens. Our word *clerical,* describing office work, can be traced back to this duty of clergymen in the Middle Ages.

A monk copying the Scriptures and a hand-copied page of the Latin Vulgate

Women also devoted their lives to the church. Those who took these vows were called *nuns.* Monks, nuns, priests, and popes still exist today. The Roman Catholic Church carries on these traditions from the Middle Ages.

The Franks

The Franks, a Germanic people, invaded Europe after the fall of Rome. Over the next several centuries, the Franks formed a kingdom. Their first king was Clovis, who conquered the last of the Romans in Gaul. A large portion of western Europe fell under his control.

Clovis divided his kingdom among his four sons just before his death. His sons and their descendants were called the *Merovingian* kings. They struggled and plotted against one another, each wanting greater control. The Merovingians' authority weakened until most of the government work was done by their palace officials.

In 732, a new leader rose up to unite the Franks. Charles was not a king but a high official in a Frankish palace. He led an army against the Muslims and defeated them at the city of Tours. This victory kept the rest of Europe free from Muslim rule. Charles was given the name *Martel,* which means "the Hammer." What type of soldier and leader would be given a name like Martel?

After Charles Martel died, his son, Pepin the Short, became the new king of the Franks. He and his descendants were called *Carolingian* kings, from the Latin word for *Charles.*

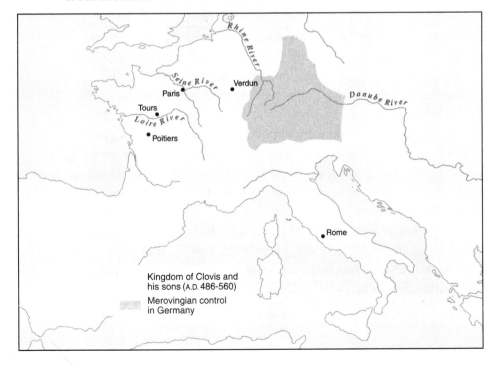

Kingdom of Clovis and his sons (A.D. 486-560)

Merovingian control in Germany

Pepin is best known for making an alliance with the church of Rome. Twelve years after Pepin became king, Pope Stephen II asked him to help defend Rome against an invader, the Lombards. In exchange for his help, the pope would officially approve Pepin's taking the Frankish crown away from the Merovingians.

In a public ceremony, Frankish bishops anointed Pepin with oil, and Pepin received the pope's blessing as king of the Franks. He went on to defeat the Lombards and to give part of their conquered land to the church leaders. The church called these lands the *Papal States,* and they remained part of Rome for centuries.

Pepin's son, Charlemagne, was the greatest of the Carolingian kings. The Latin word *magnus* means "great." Can you guess what the name *Charlemagne* means? It comes from the Latin words *Carolus Magnus,* meaning "Charles the Great."

Charlemagne

According to tradition, Charlemagne was praying beside Pope Leo III at the church service on Christmas Day in 800. The pope turned and placed a crown on Charlemagne's head, calling him emperor of the western Roman Empire.

Charlemagne had extended the Frankish kingdom to be greater in size than ever before. It was now an empire that included most of western Europe. Charlemagne divided his lands into small districts, each having several *manors,* or farms. Each manor sent Charlemagne a yearly report on its workers, production, and resources. Charlemagne regularly checked on local officials to make sure that their methods of rule were just.

Under Charlemagne's rule, the empire awakened to learning. Believing in the value of education, Charlemagne began schools for boys from both noble and poor families. These scholars studied reading, writing, mathematics, and astronomy. Charlemagne even struggled to teach himself how to read and write. He kept a tablet and a pen beneath his pillow and practiced often. Charlemagne never mastered these subjects, but he was an excellent speaker, even in the Latin language, and he learned how to make calculations.

Charlemagne even reformed handwriting in his empire. When scholars discovered that the writing in the monastery's books was hard to read, Charlemagne ordered a monk named Alcuin to develop a new style. Alcuin's writing style, which used both small and capital letters, is the basis for our handwriting today.

Charlemagne and II Timothy 2:15 written in the style he directed Alcuin to develop

Study to show thyself approved unto God, a workman that needeth not to be ashamed, rightly dividing the word of truth.

Life on the Manor

People lived on manors during the Middle Ages. The owner of a manor was called a *lord.* In the early Middle Ages, the lord lived in the manor house, usually a large house made of logs. From about the ninth century on, lords lived in castles. The lord's home was safe and strong and offered a place of protection during attacks.

The manor was like a large farm. It had woods and fishing ponds and fields where grain was grown. It also had little villages where the peasants lived.

Every manor had a church building. The people living on each manor attended the church. No one worked on Sundays. Sometimes the church celebrated other special days to honor saints or certain seasons of the year. People were released from their work for a time of feasting, dancing, and relaxation. The church called these special occasions *holy days.* What word in our language comes from this medieval term? How has the meaning of this word changed over the centuries?

The peasants who lived on the lord's land were called *serfs*. They paid rent to the lord and worked part-time for him. They farmed his land, cleared new lands, built and repaired buildings, dug ditches, and fixed roads. The lord even expected extra gifts from them at Christmas and Easter.

The serfs did not have many possessions of their own. They had to use the lord's mill to grind their grain into flour. They had to bake their bread in the lord's oven. Often the lord made them pay to use these items.

The homes of the serfs were very small. Some were only about fifteen feet long and six feet wide. Entire families ate, slept, and lived in the same room. Most serfs shared their homes with their sheep, cows, or pigs. The animals usually stayed in a separate room, partitioned off from the living area.

Serfs were bound to the same land all of their lives. They could leave only if they paid the lord.

Serfs are shown working on their lord's land in this early 15th century French illustration.

However, some peasants on manors were called *freemen* instead of serfs. They paid less rent, worked fewer hours for the lord, and were allowed to move from the manor if they wanted to.

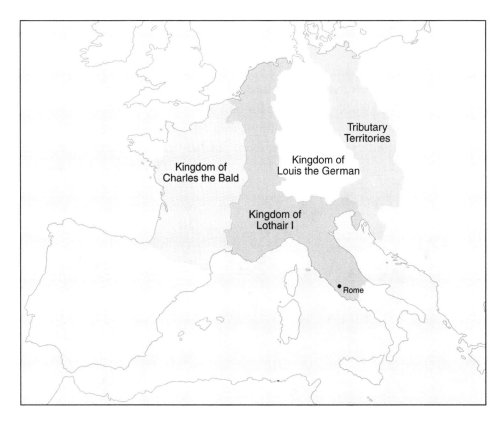

Division of Charlemagne's Empire

Charlemagne's son, Louis the Pious, inherited his father's empire. But the empire was too large for one man to rule successfully, and it soon weakened. Wars among Louis and his three sons led to a division of Charlemagne's empire into three parts. Each of Louis's sons—Lothair, Charles the Bald, and Louis the German—received a share.

Two of these three parts formed the basis for two of our modern European countries. Compare the map on this page with a map of modern Europe. Can you guess which two modern countries came from these kingdoms?

Charles the Bald's section of the empire would one day become France. Louis the German's territory would be the nation of Germany. Lothair's part of the empire, located between the territories of his brothers, would be a source of strife between France and Germany for centuries.

At the time of the division, the languages spoken in the western and eastern parts of the empire were very different from one another. Western Frankish was changing into French, and eastern Frankish was developing into German.

Vikings!

The bells in the church at Tours began to ring wildly, a shrill warning to villagers. "I've seen their ships!" cried one of the monks. "Coming down the Loire River! It's the Northmen—the Vikings! May God help us!"

Long wooden boats with curved ends sailed toward the village. Some villagers caught glimpses of the boatmen's faces. Beneath their thick, blond hair, their expressions were fierce. Even when seated, they looked tall. Strong hands gripped long oars. Fifty warriors must have been in each boat.

The attack was swift. Armed with spears, the Vikings invaded the village. They killed people, stole gold and expensive jewelry, and destroyed homes and buildings. Then, as quickly as they had come, they shoved off shore and were gone. Behind them the village lay in ruins.

This scene was a common one in Europe in the 800s. Viking raiders attacked Britain and then struck at the Franks in western Europe. They often attacked small villages, one at a time. Their attacks were always sudden and merciless, and they were feared by all.

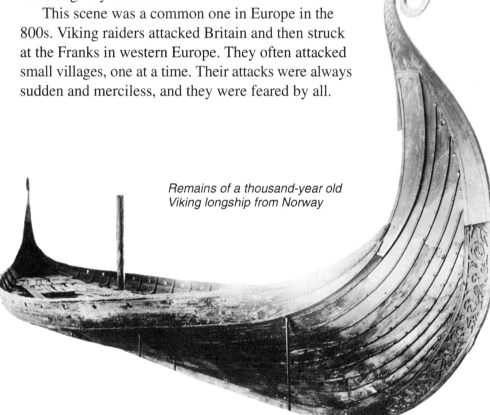

Remains of a thousand-year old Viking longship from Norway

The Names of the Days

The Vikings, often called *Norsemen* or *north men* by the Franks, were a fierce warrior people from Scandinavia. We remember them not only as raiders but also as explorers. They were the first to discover Iceland, Greenland, and the North American Atlantic coast.

An ancient Viking cart

The Norse worshiped many gods, just as the Greeks and Romans had. Their chief god was named Odin (or Wodan). They believed that Odin was the one-eyed god of war, the god of creation, and the god of the dead. Under Odin was Thor, the giant-killing god. The Norse believed that Thor had authority over the wind and rain and acted as a guardian of justice. A third god, Frey, and his twin sister, Freya, were believed to be the god and goddess of love.

Almost every day, we "echo" the names of these gods from the Norse myths. Think about the names of the days in our week. Wednesday comes from the name for the chief god, Odin (*Wodan's Day*). Thursday is named for Thor (*Thor's Day*). Can you guess where the name Friday comes from?

Feudalism

Life in Europe during the centuries after Charlemagne's death has been called the *Age of Feudalism.* Feudalism was the name for the type of government that developed during this time period.

Under the system of feudalism, two nobles entered into an agreement. One of them agreed to be the *vassal,* or servant, of the other. The vassal had to perform certain duties for the other noble, or the lord. Some of these duties included fighting for the lord in battle and providing lodging for the lord when he traveled on the vassal's land. In a special ceremony, the vassal knelt before the lord and took an oath of *fealty,* or faithfulness, promising to be loyal to the lord.

In exchange for these favors, the lord gave the vassal a *fief,* or a fee, which was usually a piece of land. Although the fief still belonged to the lord, the vassal could use it freely.

Being asked to become a vassal was considered a great honor. Vassals could, in turn, divide up their own land and become lords over lesser vassals. Divisions of land and loyalties often continued until the fief was the size of an average manor. A piece of land this size was large enough to support one knight.

Have you seen pictures or read stories about knights? The knight was a mounted soldier who defended the manor during the Middle Ages. He wore a suit of metal armor from head to foot, and his horse was also heavily armored. He carried a sword, a lance, and sometimes a battle-ax as weapons. He wielded a heavy shield to protect himself in battle.

Nearly any nobleman could become a knight if he proved himself worthy. He had to be faithful and skilled in warfare. A young boy who wanted to be a knight could take the first step at the age of seven by becoming a *page*. As a page, a boy went to live in the castle of another noble to learn horsemanship and fighting skills. He also did chores for the lord and lady of the castle. At fourteen, he became a *squire*. His responsibilities then included helping his master dress, accompanying him on hunts or into battles, and caring for his warhorse. He continued his lessons in bow, sword, and lance fighting. When he was twenty-one, he could become a knight.

An elaborate ceremony was necessary for a man to become a knight. Before this ceremony, the man spent the entire night in church, praying that he would be worthy of the honor.

The next morning, other knights solemnly dressed him in his armor. The knight knelt before his lord, who touched him on the shoulder with a sword and said, "I dub you knight."

Sometimes new knights went immediately into battle. When there were no battles going on, knights often planned mock battles called *tournaments.* Rival groups of knights met to have *jousting* contests. The goal of a joust was for one knight to knock the other off his horse with a blunt lance. Great honor went to the winning jouster.

While a knight was fighting, the only way to identify him was by his coat of arms. The coat of arms was the emblem painted on his shield, and each knight had a different coat of arms.

What kind of person do you imagine when you think of a knight? How would he act in danger, or how would he treat a lady? Knights of the Middle Ages lived by a code of behavior called *chivalry.* This code taught a knight to be generous, loyal to his lord, skillful and brave in battle, faithful to the Roman Church, and protective of women. Do you think many knights lived up to these standards of chivalry?

The Battle of Hastings

In 1066, the king of England died without an heir. Two powerful nobles, Harold Godwinson and Duke William of Normandy, both claimed the throne. Harold set himself up as the next king of England. William called upon his vassals to provide him with men and supplies to form an army. William and his army met Harold's forces on a field near the town of Hastings.

Harold, wanting to force William to attack first, placed his men along the top of a ridge. Standing side-by-side, Harold's men formed a *shield wall.* William knew his men would have to break through this wall to win the battle.

William and the Norman army surged up the hill toward Harold's men. Shouts rang out and metal clanged as the two armies clashed. William's army attacked the shield wall again and again. Late in the afternoon, the Norman army finally broke through. Harold was killed in the fierce struggle, and soon afterward his army fled.

William was now the king of England. He chose some of his own men to be lords, replacing the ones who were not loyal to him. All of England became a feudal kingdom. William was called "William the Conqueror."

One of many scenes on the Bayeaux Tapestry depicting the Battle of Hastings

The Castle

Castles had become common in Europe by the eleventh century. The castle in the Middle Ages was both a home and a military fortress.

Castles were surrounded by strong walls. Some castles in the later Middle Ages had stone walls over thirty feet thick. Inside the walls were towers, halls, and the courtyard.

The lord and his family had their living quarters in the keep. The keep, an inner castle tower, was the safest place in the castle. Often the keep stood on a hill. Inside it were the great hall, where meetings and banquets were held; the kitchen; the family's bedrooms and sitting rooms; and a few other rooms, such as offices or a chapel. Servants often slept in the rooms where they worked, rather than having private bedrooms.

Castles were cold and dark inside. Lords tried to brighten them by painting the walls and ceilings with bright colors and placing burning torches in the rooms. They put mats on the floors and hung large woven tapestries on the walls to keep out the cold.

Medieval tapestry, ca. A.D. 1500

The Metropolitan Museum of Art, Gift of John D. Rockefeller Jr., 1937
Photograph © 1988 The Metropolitan Museum of Art

Giving Medieval Banquets

Wealthy people liked to give large banquets during the Middle Ages. Lords would invite many guests, and they would eat at long tables in the great hall of the castle. Pages waited on tables. Squires were often responsible to carve the meat for the guests.

Many different foods were served at these banquets. One meal might have included soup, cheese made from a pig's head, puddings, baked fish, pork, venison, pheasants, larks, and other birds. Dessert was usually a pie filled with fish or fowl. Have you ever heard the nursery rhyme that tells of "four and twenty blackbirds baked in a pie"? One medieval custom was to insert live birds into a pie and release them in front of the guests when dessert was served.

Banquet guests used large, flat pieces of bread as plates. Forks were never used until the 1600s, so the guests used their fingers to eat most foods. But they still observed certain rules about table manners. No one was supposed to gnaw on the bones, and it was considered rude to dip food into the common salt bowl.

Early castles were made of wood. By the twelfth century, most castles were made of thick stone. Builders dug *moats,* wide trenches filled with water, around the castle to keep attackers from reaching it easily. A *drawbridge* crossed the moat to the castle gate. During an attack, the castle guards raised the drawbridge to cover the gate, cutting off the entrance to the castle.

If attackers got safely across the moat, they had to face the *gatehouse.* The gatehouse was a large stronghold in the castle wall. If the attackers entered the gatehouse, castle defenders could lower a large screen to trap them inside.

Soldiers attacked castles in different ways. Sometimes they used a *battering ram,* a long log tipped with iron, to knock down the gate or part of the castle wall. Sometimes they built tall towers, rolled them up against the wall, and climbed over into the castle. Sometimes they threw rocks and burning rags into the courtyard. And sometimes they dug tunnels beneath the castle, started fires in the tunnels, and tried to burn away the foundation so that the castle would collapse.

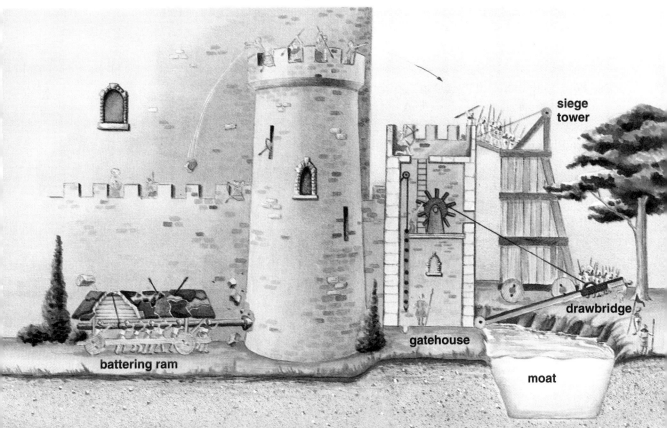

siege tower

drawbridge

gatehouse

battering ram

moat

Henry's Legal System

In 1154, after many years of civil war, Henry II came to power in England. He developed England's legal system, extending the king's power into new areas.

The courts of Henry's day tried people suspected of crimes by *ordeal.* A common method of trial by ordeal was to tie an accused person's hands and feet with rope and throw him into deep water. The people believed that if he floated, the pure water had "rejected" him because of his sin, and he was considered guilty; if he sank, he was innocent. What do you think usually happened to the "innocent" person?

After the civil wars, many land claims had to be settled, and the courts that tried by ordeal could not be used for this purpose. Henry II developed new procedures. He issued *writs,* or royal orders, to the local sheriffs, instructing them to decide who actually held each piece of disputed land. Even though someone else may have owned the land, the person who actually lived on it got to keep it. The sheriffs' decisions required *juries.* Jury members were local people who came to the court to tell what they knew about who had the best claim to the land.

If the sheriff gave a writ to someone who disagreed with the land settlement, that person could return the writ to the sheriff. A new court case then decided whether the first decision of the sheriff was correct. When a particularly difficult case came up, it was sent directly to Henry II for his decision. Over time, such decisions were written down and enforced throughout England, becoming England's common law.

A Jury Works

1. Listen as your teacher tells you which role you will play in the mock trial.

2. Follow your teacher's instructions as the trial proceeds.

3. Discuss the trial with your classmates. Was enough evidence given? Was the jury fair in its decision? How is this kind of trial superior to a trial by ordeal?

The scepter (above) and orb (below) of the Holy Roman Emperors

Henry II's family, called the *Plantagenets,* ruled England until the end of the 1400s. A family called the *Capets* ruled France during this time. Germany and most of Italy made up the Holy Roman Empire, an empire under the joint control of an emperor and the pope of the Roman Catholic Church. The Byzantine Empire was thriving in Eastern Europe.

The Crusades did much to weaken the system of feudalism. Fighting in Crusades was expensive, and most of the money was furnished by individual lords. Some lords even had to sell or mortgage their properties to pay for their Crusade expenses. Also, many serfs left their manors to fight in the Crusades. Most who left, having tasted freedom, never returned.

"The Lord is my rock, and my fortress, and my deliverer; my God, my strength, in whom I will trust; my buckler, and the horn of my salvation, and my high tower."

Psalm 18:2

By the year 1500, central governments all over Europe were run by kings. England and France were well on their way to becoming strong nations. The medieval world was no more. The modern era of history was about to begin.

Glossary

abacus a wooden frame with rows of movable beads used to make mathematical calculations

acupuncture a method of relieving pain by sticking needles into certain points of the body

A.D. an abbreviation for the Latin words *anno Domini,* which mean "in the year of the Lord"; used in giving dates after the birth of Christ

agora a marketplace in ancient Greece

ambergris a waxy substance obtained from whales; used in perfumes

amphitheater an outdoor theater which consists of a stage or arena surrounded by rows of seats, each row higher and farther back than the row in front of it

ancestor worship the religious practice that includes prayers to dead ancestors to try to please and receive blessings from them

aqueduct a raised trough that carried water through a city

arch an open, curved structure that supports the weight of the building material on top of it

archaeologist a person who studies ancient societies and the way of life and customs of their people

architecture the skill or business of designing and planning buildings or a style or special method of building

artifact an object from the past that reveals something about the people and culture in which it was made

artisans workers who turn raw materials into finished goods

Bantu an early African people

barbarian name given by the Romans to nomadic peoples

barrel vault several arches placed back-to-back to form a tunnel

batab the man in charge of the Mayan armies

battering ram a long log tipped with iron used to attack castle gates and walls

B.C. an abbreviation for the words *Before Christ*; used in giving dates before the birth of Christ

block printing a method of printing that uses carved letters and words and ink, working as a rubber stamp does; first used by the Chinese during the Golden Age

botanists people who study plants

bronze a hard metal made of copper and tin and sometimes other elements; first developed by the ancient Chinese

Buddha the title of a religious leader, Siddhartha Gautama, that means "Enlightened One"; he began the religion of Buddhism

caesar the ruler of a state

caesaropapism occurs when a ruler claims to have authority over the empire and the church

calligraphy a type of writing done with a paintbrush and smooth strokes, originating in China

caste social class

catacombs underground tombs

causeway land bridge

character a symbol used in writing, such as a letter or a pictograph

chivalry a code of behavior

city-state an independent city and its surrounding land

clan a group of people who claim to have a common ancestor

classic an artist, writer, or object thought to be the best of its kind

clergy religious leaders

comedy one type of Greek drama designed to make the audience laugh and to put them in a lighthearted mood

composure control over one's emotions; a calm manner; self-control

compound a set of huts or houses in ancient India usually belonging to one family

concrete a mixture of gravel and sand in mortar; first used by the Romans

Confucius a scholar and teacher who greatly influenced ancient China; his teachings are called the Confucian *Classics*

consuls those who governed the Roman Senate

covenant a promise or agreement made between two or more persons; an agreement between God and man

crusade any of the military expeditions that European Christians undertook in the eleventh, twelfth, and thirteenth centuries to take the Holy Land from the Muslims; any campaign or movement for reform, a cause, or an ideal

cuneiform word meaning "wedge-shaped" that refers to the Sumerian writing

cylinder a hollow or solid object shaped like a tube, pipe, or tree trunk

delta a mass of sand, mud, and soil that settles at the mouth of a river and is often shaped like a fan or a triangle

democracy a form of government in which the decisions are made directly by the people

dialogues books by Plato written in the form of conversations

Diaspora the scattering of the Jews into other countries after Nebuchadnezzar conquered Judah

dig excavation

dome a large, rounded roof that fits on a round base, looking like an upside-down bowl

drawbridge a bridge that can be raised or turned to prevent someone from crossing it or to permit boats to pass through

drought a long period with little or no rain

dynasty a line of kings or rulers who belong to the same family

embalmer one who preserves a body by using special treatments

Epicureanism a belief that there is no God, that no life after death exists, and that the present is all that matters; people who believed this lived for pleasure and tried to stay happy and free from pain

etiquette a set of rules that tell you how to behave in various social situations

excavate to dig or dig out; to uncover by digging

exile forced removal from one's country; a banishing; a person who has been forced to leave his country

exports goods sent to another country for trade or sale

famine a bad shortage of food in an area

fealty faithfulness and loyalty

fief a fee, which was usually a piece of land

fjord a narrow inlet from the sea

flax a plant with blue flowers and slender stems that make a fiber used to make cloth

Forum the Roman marketplace

Fujiwara a family who ruled Japan during the Golden Age

gatehouse a large stronghold in the castle wall

gladiator a professional fighter in Rome

golden age a time when a country is at its best

Gregorian calendar the calendar in use today; a reformed version of one used in ancient Rome

guild a union of merchants or craftsmen in the Middle Ages

guru a Hindu teacher

haiku a Japanese poem consisting of three lines with words chosen according to meaning and syllables; the entire poem contains seventeen syllables

headman the most important man in the ancient Indian village

Hebrews the Jewish people of ancient times; the Israelites

hieroglyphics Egyptian picture writing

Hinduism a religion that originated in ancient India; involves the worship of thousands of gods and includes a belief in reincarnation and a deity in nature

hippodrome a large open-air stadium in ancient Rome

holy days special occasions

Hyksos a people who invaded Egypt using horse-drawn chariots

icon a sacred picture or statue of Jesus or the saints

iconoclasm hatred of icons

iconoclast one who dislikes icons

ides of March the fifteenth day of March

ikebana a special Japanese art form that involved arranging flowers

Indian subcontinent the section of Asia cut off from the rest of the continent by the Himalaya Mountains; consists of India and some of its neighbors

infidels those people who did not believe the Islam religion during the Byzantine Empire

initiation ceremony a special service in ancient India that celebrated a Hindu boy becoming a man, symbolized by a sacred cord that was hung over his shoulder

Islam the religion of Muslims, who believe that Allah is the only god and Muhammad is his prophet

jihad a holy war fought for the Islamic faith

joust a combat between two knights on horses

judges deliverers sent by God to bring peace to the Hebrews

Julian calendar the calendar designed by Julius Caesar; became the basis for the modern calendar

jury a group of citizens sworn to hear the facts and evidence on cases presented in a court of law

Kaaba a temple in Mecca where thousands of Arabs came to worship during the time of the Byzantine Empire

keep an inner castle tower where the lord and his family lived

Koran an Islamic holy book that supposedly contains messages given to Muhammad from Allah

lacquer a clear and shiny coating

landscape painting a type of painting commonly done by the ancient Chinese on silk or paper scrolls; usually depicted a scene of nature

lapis lazuli a bright blue stone used by Mesopotamian artisans

law a rule made by a government for the people living in a country, state, city, or town; a set of such rules

legionary a soldier in Rome's infantry

legions units of several thousand men that made up Rome's infantry

linguist a person who studies languages and the ways they change

linguistics the study of languages

lord owner of a manor

lyre a small harp

makina the "great sun lord"

mandarin an official who helped the Han rulers govern the country and was chosen after long years of studying and difficult testing

manor farm

medieval middle age

mercenaries soldiers who fight for pay

metaphor a word symbol used in literature

migrating moving from region to region

minaret a tower on a mosque

moat a wide trench filled with water, usually surrounding a castle

monarchy rule by one

monastery a building or set of buildings where monks live and work in a group

monk a member of a men's religious order who lives in a monastery and observes the rules of that order

monsoon a strong wind that brings heavy rain

mosaic a picture made of small stones or pieces of glass

mummy a preserved body treated with special ointments and wrapped in linen bandages

muses a group of nine Greek goddesses that presided over the arts

Muslim a person who believes in the religion of Islam

myth a legend or traditional story that expresses what a people believes and values; often involves ancestors, heroes, or gods

nanna the moon god

natron a salt solution

natural barriers landforms that isolate a country from outside influence

nilometer a device used by the ancient Egyptians that measured the height of the river after a flood

nomad wanderer

north men "Norsemen," or Vikings

nun a woman who devotes her life to the Roman Catholic Church

Old Kingdom the name given to Egypt after it was united by Narmer in 3100 B.C.

oligarchy rule by a few

optical illusion occurs when an object appears to take a shape it does not really have

oracle a message given by a person who was supposedly a prophet or a god

orator speaker

ordeal a painful or dangerous situation

outcaste one who was outside the social caste system in India; an untouchable

pack a group of boys who lived together and trained for war in ancient Sparta

page a boy who served a knight

pagoda a Chinese tower usually used as a temple or shrine; originated during the Tang dynasty

pantheism the belief that there is deity in nature

Pantheon a temple; the largest domed building in Rome that is still standing today, rising fourteen stories high

papal pertains to the pope

papyrus paper made from the stalk of the papyrus plant, a reed that grows along the banks of the Nile

Parthenon an enormous Greek temple on the Acropolis that was made of white marble and dedicated to the goddess Athena

Passover a Jewish festival that lasts eight days in celebration of their escape from Egypt and the sparing of their first-born children when the Egyptians' first-born were killed

Patriarch the leader of the Eastern Orthodox Church

patrician a member of the noble class in Rome

Pax Romana "Peace of Rome"

pedagogue a servant who accompanied wealthy Greek boys to school to make sure they behaved; now refers to a teacher

pendulum a weight hung by a light cord, chain, or bar so that it can easily swing back and forth

pharaoh the king of Egypt

Pharisees Jewish religious leaders who stressed complete obedience to the Law

Philistines Israel's worst enemies

philosopher a scholar who tries to define the meaning of life; the word means "lover of wisdom"

Phoenicians those who lived in Phoenicia, an ancient country at the eastern end of the Mediterranean Sea

pictographs pictures used in place of words

pilgrimage a religious journey to a shrine or temple

plague a deadly disease that spreads rapidly from person to person

plebeian a member of the common social class in Rome; consisted of laborers, farmers, artisans, merchants, and foreigners

pok-to-pok a Mayan ball game

polytheism the worship of many gods

pope the bishop of the church of Rome

porcelain a hard, white kind of china made by baking fine clay at a high temperature

porch an open-air building in the Greek marketplace

porter a man who carried goods to market

pozole a favorite Mayan drink made from corn paste and water, sometimes mixed with honey

proverb a wise saying

Punic Wars the three major wars between Rome and Carthage

Purim a Jewish holiday that celebrates Haman's death and the deliverance of the Jewish people

rain shadow an area that receives no rain because it lies beyond another area where water vapor is blown

reincarnation the Hindu belief that the soul, after death, takes another body, sometimes in the form of another human or an animal

republic a form of government in which the power rests with the people who elect representatives to govern the country

rhetoric persuasive language

sacraments Roman Catholic ceremonies that are believed to bring salvation

Sadducees Jewish religious leaders who made allowances for the ideas and customs of the secular rulers of Israel

Sanskrit Indian writing

savanna grassland

school-father chief teacher

scientific method a method of study requiring careful observation and record keeping

scribe a person who copied books, letters, and other kinds of written material before printing was invented

seismograph an instrument that is used to detect and measure earthquakes

Senate the governing body of the Roman patricians

serf a peasant who lived on the lord's land

shadoof a long pole with a weight on one end and a bucket on the other

shell inlay a craft of the Mesopotamians that contained white shells pressed into softened tar to make a design

Shintoism the main religion of Japan; includes emperor worship

Silk Road a trade route that crossed many of China's natural barriers and stretched for over four thousand miles to the west

sistrum an instrument made of metal rods attached to a metal frame and used during Egyptian celebrations

squire a young man of noble birth who served as an attendant to a knight

steatite a type of soapstone used to make Indian seals

Stoicism the Greek philosophy that duty is all that matters in life, emphasizing bravery and obedience to laws

stylus a sharp tool used for writing on clay or wax tablets

swastika means "a sign of good luck" and refers to a symbol used by the ancient Indians and later by Hitler

synagogue a building or place used by Jews for worship and religious instruction

tabernacle a place where the Israelites worshiped; a symbol of God's presence with His people

tablet-house a Sumerian school building

tamale chopped and spiced meat rolled in cornmeal and cooked in corn husks; originated with the ancient Mayas

tell mound

terra cotta a type of clay

theocracy a government led by religious authority; direct rule by God

theorem a carefully tested idea

ting a special bronze vessel made by the Shang and used to cook meat as a sacrifice

toga one-piece robe

Torah the first five books of the Bible claimed as the Jewish law

tortilla a round, flat bread made from cornmeal or flour and water; originated by the Mayas

tournament a contest among several persons or teams in which they compete until one team is declared the winner

tragedy one type of Greek drama designed to instruct, usually ending with the downfall of the hero because of some character flaw

treaty peace agreement

tribune a leader of the Greek plebeian Assembly

tribute taxes paid to a ruler by conquered peoples

tyrant a ruler who uses power unjustly or cruelly; any person who is unjust and cruel

untouchable an Indian who was outside the caste system

vassal servant

Vedas sacred books of Hinduism

veto the right or power to keep a proposed law from becoming a law

vina a type of lute similar to a guitar

vizier the second highest official in the Egyptian government

Yahweh Jehovah

ziggurat a temple tower in ancient Ur

zimbabwe a large stone house built by the ancient Shona in Africa

Index

A

Abraham, 2, 6-7, 13, 17, 50, 52-53
Acropolis, 128, 131
Adriatic Sea, 254
Aegean Sea, 121-22, 245, 265
Ahasuerus, 65
Alexander the Great, 66, 141-42, 144, 154
Alexius I Comnenus, 264
Alps, 148, 153, 234
Amenhotep II, 41
Amenhotep IV, 45
Antioch, 256
Arabian Peninsula, 259
Arabic numerals, 237
archaeology, 2, 4-6, 12, 17-18, 42, 75, 79-80, 86, 102, 172, 177, 195, 199, 206. *See also* artifacts
architecture, 4, 15, 18, 20, 120, 128, 131-32, 134, 138, 144, 147, 163-64, 168, 174, 225, 233, 242, 251
Aristotle, 136, 141
artifacts, 4, 6, 34, 75, 79-86, 88, 178, 215. *See also* archaeology
Asia Minor, 43, 245-46, 254-55, 261, 267-69
Assembly, 124, 149-51, 162
Assyria, 63
Athens, 123-25, 128-29, 131-32, 136, 141, 143, 245
Augustus, 162, 165-66

B

Babylon, 64-66
Bangladesh, 78
barbarians, 247-48, 254-55, 260
Beirut, 256
Belgium, 157
Bethlehem, 166
Black Death, 269
Black Sea, 244-45, 254
Britain. 70, 157. *See also* England
Buddha, 95, 218, 225-27, 235, 241
Burma, 78, 99
Byzantium, 206, 243-45, 247-48, 254, 256, 259, 262, 264-65, 267-69

C

calligraphy, 225, 233
Canaan, 39, 50-52, 54, 57-58, 61-62
Carolus Magnus, 278
Carthage, 152-54, 248
Charlemagne, 278-79, 282, 285
Charles Martel, 277
Ch'in. *See* Qin Shi Huangdi
China, 78, 97-100, 103-4, 106, 108, 117-18, 214-16, 218-20, 222, 224-28, 233-35, 242, 245, 256
Cicero, 161
Classical Age, 104, 120, 123, 136, 240
Columbus, Christopher, 170
Confucius, 104-6, 111, 118, 219
Constantine, 206, 247, 269

Constantinople, 131, 247,
250-51, 256, 261-69
crusades, 264-67, 270, 294
cuneiform, 10
Cyrus the Great, 66

D

Daniel, 64
Dark Ages, 123-24, 134
David, 62-64
de Landa, Diego, 178-79
Dead Sea, 51, 71
Denmark, 274
Diocletian, 167-68

E

Eastern Orthodox Church, 262,
265, 268
Egypt, 9, 23, 25-28, 30-31, 35,
37-48, 52-54, 64, 206, 212, 248,
255, 259, 264-65, 267
England, 77, 96, 269, 283, 288,
294. *See also* Britain
Esther, 65
Ethiopia, 193, 206
Euphrates River, 2-3, 7, 9, 41
Ezekiel, 62

F

Far East, 99, 214
feudalism, 285, 288, 294
Finland, 274
France, 157, 249, 269, 272, 282,
294

G

Gaul, 157, 273, 277
Germany, 88, 157, 282, 294

Golden Age, 213-20, 222-23,
225-27, 230, 235-37, 239, 242,
263
Great Pyramid, 33
Great Wall, 109
Greece, 119-23, 126-27, 130,
133-38, 141, 144, 154, 168,
170, 254, 269
Greenland, 284
Gregorian calendar, 159
Gregory III, 262

H

Hagia Sophia, 251, 267, 269
Haman, 65
Hannibal, 153-54
Hanukkah, 67
Hebrews, 40-41, 52-53, 57
Henry II, 292, 294
Heraclius, 255-56, 259
Herodotus, 137
hieroglyphics, 35-36
Himalaya Mountains, 78
Hittites, 43
Holland, 157

I

Iceland, 274, 284
icons, 262, 269
India, 70, 73, 75-78, 81, 86-89,
91, 93, 95-96, 99, 170, 205,
214, 235-37, 239, 242, 245
Indian Ocean, 78, 194
Innocent III, 265
Iran, 3
Iraq, 2-3
Isaac, 6, 50, 52-53

Israel, 50-53, 56-58, 60-63, 68, 72

Italy, 146-48, 152-54, 157, 161, 249, 273, 294

J

Jacob, 39, 52-53

Japan, 214, 226-28, 230, 234-35, 242

Jeroboam, 63

Jerusalem, 61-64, 66-67, 70, 259, 264

Jordan, 3, 51

Jordan River, 51

Joseph, 38-40, 52

Joshua, 57

Judah Maccabeus, 67

Julian calendar, 159

Julius Caesar, 156-60, 162

Justinian I, 248-51, 254

K

Kenya, 204

Khufu, 33

Korea, 234

Kuwait, 3

L

Laos, 99

Latins, 147

Lebanon, 51, 61-62

Leo III, 260-62, 279

Libya, 27

M

Madagascar, 194

Mansa Musa, 211

Mark Antony, 161

Masada, 70-72

Masai, 204

Mayas, 169-75, 177-79, 181-82, 185-87, 190-94, 237

Mecca, 211, 257-58

Mediterranean Sea, 27, 29, 51, 121, 124, 148, 152, 154, 245, 248, 265

Memphis, 34

Mesopotamia, 1-3, 7, 20

Mexico, 170, 172-73

Michael VIII, 267-68

Middle Ages, 34, 132, 271-72, 275-76, 280, 286-87, 289-90

Moab, 64

Mohenjo-Daro, 74-75, 77, 79, 81, 85-86, 96

Mongolia, 99

Mordecai, 65

Morocco, 212

Moses, 41, 52-54, 56-57

Mount Ararat, 246

Mount Fuji, 234

Mount Kilimanjaro, 196

Mount Sinai, 54

Muhammad, 257-59, 261, 269

N

Nazareth, 166

Nebuchadnezzar, 62, 64

Nero, 167

New Testament, 144

Nicaea, 267

Nile River, 23-31, 34-35, 37, 46-48, 52, 193

Noah, 6

North Korea, 99

Norway, 274

O

Octavian, 162-64
Old Testament, 166
Olympic Games, 135
Omar, 259
Orient, 213-14, 217, 242

P

Pacific Ocean, 99, 234
Pakistan, 78-79, 99
Palestine, 41, 255
Pantheon, 164
Parthenon, 131-32
Paul the Apostle, 34, 143
Pax Romana, 162-66, 168
Peloponnesian War, 141
Pepin the Short, 277-78
Pericles, 128
Persia, 66, 215, 255, 259
Persian Wars, 128, 141
Phoenicia, 61-62
Plato, 136
Pompey, 157, 160
Potiphar, 38
Punic Wars, 152-54
Purim, 65

Q

Qin Shi Huangdi, 108-11

R

Ramses II, 43
Red Sea, 27, 41
Rehoboam, 63
Renaissance, 272
Roman Catholic Church, 178,
  194, 262, 265, 275-76, 287, 294

Roman Empire, 248-49, 256,
  272-73, 279, 294
Rome, 22, 70, 144, 146-47,
  149-50, 152-65, 167-68, 170,
  206, 262, 264, 268, 272-73, 275
Rosetta stone, 35
Russia, 99, 264

S

Samaria, 63-64
Samuel, 57
Saudi Arabia, 3
Saul, 60-61
Scandinavia, 273-74, 284
Sesostris II, 38-39
Shona (Mashona), 213
Siddhartha Gautama. *See*
  Buddha
Socrates, 136
Solomon, 61-63
Somalia, 193-94
Songhai, 207, 212-13
Spain, 153, 157, 212, 273
Sparta, 123, 125, 141
Sphinx, 25, 33-34
Sudan, 27, 37, 41, 204, 207
Sumer, 2, 4, 6-10, 12-19, 21-22
Sweden, 274
Switzerland, 157
Syria, 3, 41, 51, 67, 253, 255,
  259, 264

T

Tanzania, 196, 204
Tigris River, 2-3, 7
Timbuktu, 212
Titus, 70

Turkey, 3, 246
Tutankhamen, 42, 45
Tyre, 62, 256

U
Uganda, 204
Ur, 2, 6-7, 9, 12-18, 20
Urban II, 264

V
Vespasian, 70
Vietnam, 99

W
William the Conqueror, 288

X
Xerxes, 127-28

Z
Zimbabwe, 213

Photograph Credits

The following agencies and individuals have furnished materials to meet the photographic needs of this textbook. We wish to express our gratitude to them for their important contribution.

Carl Abrams
Ward Andersen
Aramco World Magazine
Art Resource
Austrian Press and Information Service
Gary Balius
Chris Barton
Bowater, Inc.
The British Library
The British Museum
Cadbury Ltd.
B. W. Carper
Christie's Images
Christine Osborne Pictures
George R. Collins
Corbis-Bettmann
Corel Corporation
Stewart Custer
Terry M. Davenport
Egyptian Tourist Authority
Gene Fisher
J. A. Franklin
Freer Gallery of Art
French Government Tourist Office
Friends of Free China
Greek National Tourist Organization

Greenville Public Library
Grace Collins Hargis
Peggy E. Hargis
India Tourist Office
Annie Lee Jones
Lyndia Jones
Sivasankar Kumar Kande
Mary Kraus
Kunsthistorisches, Museum Vienna
Library of Congress
Mary Evans Picture Library
Metropolitan Museum of Art
Mexican Government Tourism Office
National Archives
National Gallery of Art
Norwegian Tourist Board
Science and Society Picture Library
Stock Montage
Turkish Ministry of Tourism
Unusual Films
Vatican Museum
Harry Ward
West Point Museum
World Bank
Xinhua News Agency

Cover
World Bank (farmer, sheep); Ward Andersen (cistern, Parthenon)

Title Page
Aramco World Magazine

Chapter 1
John Feeney/Aramco World 1; Metropolitan Museum of Art 2 (left); Unusual Films 2 (right), 4 (right), 8 (top left), 10 (both), 11, 15 (both), 17 (all), 21; Aramco World Magazine 4 (left), 8 (top right); The Bob Jones University Collection and the Bowen Bible Lands Museum 4 (inset); Annie Lee Jones 5 (all); World Bank 8 (bottom); Wendy Levine/Aramco World 13 (top); Corel Corporation 13 (bottom); Corbis-Bettmann 14; Scala/Art Resource, NY 16

Chapter 2

Aramco World Magazine 23, 34, 48; Corel Corporation 25, 26 (bottom), 42 (bottom left, top right), 43 (middle, right); Torben B. Larsen/Aramco World 26 (top); Kunsthistorisches, Museum Vienna 30; Gene Fisher 32; Unusual Films 33 (top), 36; Harry Ward 33 (bottom); The British Museum 35 (top); Tor Eigeland/Aramco World 35 (bottom); Metropolitan Museum of Art 37; David Melody/Aramco World 40; Egyptian Tourist Authority 42 (top left, bottom right); Unusual Films 43 (left); Corbis-Bettmann 45

Chapter 3

Ward Andersen 49, 70 (inset), 72 (all); Corbis-Bettmann 53; Unusual Films 55, 59, 62 (both), 64, 71; Lyndia Jones 56, 69

Chapter 4

Peggy E. Hargis 73, 87, 89 (bottom); Christine Osborne Pictures 75, 80; World Bank 79 (photo by Kay Muldoon), 90 (bottom photo by Witlin); Unusual Films 83, 89 (top); National Archives 88; Greenville Public Library 90 (top); Sivasankar Kumar Kande 91 (all), 92 (both); Christie's Images 94; Government of India Tourist Office 95

Chapter 5

Mary Kraus 97, 98 (right), 100 (left), 109 (left); Gary Balius 98 (left), 100 (right), 105, 118 (both); Freer Gallery of Art, Smithsonian Institution, Washington, DC; Purchase, F1960.18 101(left); Freer Gallery of Art, Smithsonian Institution, Washington, DC; Purchase, F1938.5 101(right); Freer Gallery of Art, Smithsonian Institution, Washington, DC; Gift of Eugene and Agnes E. Meyer, F1961.30 107 (top right); Unusual Films 103, 107 (bottom), 113, 116 (both); Library of Congress 104; Metropolitan Museum of Art 107 (top left); Corel Corporation 109 (right); Xinhua News Agency 110; Science Museum/ Science and Society Picture Library 114; Aramco World Magazine 115 (top); Bowater, Inc. 115 (bottom)

Chapter 6

Ward Andersen 119, 143; Greek National Tourist Organization 120; West Point Museum 125; Library of Congress 128, 141; Corel Corporation 129, 139 (left); Unusual Films 132 (both), 140, 144; Vatican Museum 136; Metropolitan Museum of Art 138 (top both); Harry Ward 138 (bottom left); Stewart Custer 138 (bottom right); Christie's Images 139 (right)

Chapter 7

Ward Andersen 145, 155 (both), 168 (all); Christie's Images 147; Corbis-Bettmann 150, 156, 157, 161, 164 (bottom); Unusual Films 151, 160, 162, 166; Aramco World Magazine 153; Greenville Public Library 164 (top); Corel Corporation 165 (both); Grace Collins Hargis 167 (left); Mary Evans Picture Library 167 (right)

Chapter 8

Mexican Government Tourism Office 169, 172, 174 (both), 176, 179, 183, 184, 186, 188, 189; Unusual Films 171 (top left), 190; Cadbury Ltd. 171 (bottom left, right); Corel Corporation 177 (both); Library of Congress 187 (right)

Chapter 9

J. A. Franklin 191, 193 (bottom), 204 (both); Corel Corporation 193 (top), 195 (top right), 197 (top), 198 (both), 209 (both), 212; Unusual Films 195 (bottom right); Carl Abrams 195 (left), 201 (top), 205; Aramco World Magazine 197 (bottom); B. W. Carper 199 (top); Terry M. Davenport 199 (bottom); Chris Barton 201 (bottom), 208; Graphic House/Corbis-Bettmann 203; Brynn Bruijn/Aramco World 206; George R. Collins 210; Library of Congress 211

Chapter 10

Unusual Films 213, 219 (all), 222, 224-25 (bottom), 229, 230, 232 (all), 233 (both); Freer Gallery of Art, Smithsonian Institution, Washington, DC; Purchase, F1960.29 215; Mary Kraus 216 (top); Metropolitan Museum of Art 216 (middle); Gary Balius 216 (bottom); Corel Corporation 217, 225 (top), 226 (both), 227 (both); by permission of The British Library, Reference Number OR8210/P2 218; Freer Gallery of Art, Smithsonian Institution, Washington, DC; Gift of Charles Lang Freer, F1919.90 223; Friends of Free China 224 (top); Werner Forman/Art Resource, NY 228; Christie's Images 231; Borromeo/Art Resource, NY 241; Peggy E. Hargis 242

Chapter 11

Aramco World Magazine 243, 257, 258 (both); Turkish Ministry of Tourism 251 (both); Unusual Films 252; Library of Congress 256; Stock Montage 247, 250; Ward Andersen 259; National Gallery of Art 262; Metropolitan Museum of Art 268

Chapter 12

Library of Congress 271; Corel Corporation 272; Unusual Films 276, 293; Corbis-Bettmann 281, 290; Norwegian Tourist Board 283; French Government Tourist Office 288; Metropolitan Museum of Art 289; Austrian Press and Information Service, New York 294 (both)